Come & See

The Bible Reading Fellowship
15 The Chambers, Vineyard
Abingdon OX14 3FE
brf.org.uk

The Bible Reading Fellowship (BRF) is a Registered Charity (233280)

ISBN 978 1 80039 019 5
First published 2003 under the title *On This Rock*
First revised edition published 2011
This new edition first published 2020
Reprinted 2021
10 9 8 7 6 5 4 3 2 1
All rights reserved

Acknowledgements
Scripture quotations are from The New Revised Standard Version of the Bible,
Anglicised edition, copyright © 1989, 1995 by the Division of Christian Education
of the National Council of the Churches of Christ in the United States of America.
Used by permission. All rights reserved.

Every effort has been made to trace and contact copyright owners for material
used in this resource. We apologise for any inadvertent omissions or errors, and
would ask those concerned to contact us so that full acknowledgement can be
made in the future.

A catalogue record for this book is available from the British Library

Printed and bound in the UK by Zenith Media NP4 0DQ

Come & See

Learning from the life of Peter

Stephen Cottrell

Contents

WEEK THREE: THE WAY OF THE CROSS

WEEK FOUR: ENDURING HOPE

Acknowledgement

I would like to thank John and Anne Thomson
for their help in preparing the Bible readings for this book.

Preface

We Christians believe that the Bible tells the great story of God's love for the world he has made and for the people he has called. This story reaches its climax in Jesus, who is the one who leads us to God.

For many people growing up in Britain today, however, it is not self-evident that Jesus is the way to God. In fact, there are a great many people who do not know very much about Jesus at all. They have not been to church. They do not own a Bible and, apart from a few stories that are still told in school, they do not know the great sweep of the Bible story that is the bedrock of the Christian faith and has shaped the whole of our culture. For them, the Bible can seem old-fashioned and irrelevant. If they want to know God or find meaning in life or explore a spiritual dimension to life (and lots of people do want to do this nowadays), there is a whole smorgasbord of other tantalising treats on offer. Often, these alternatives seem more appealing. They are usually less demanding. For many people, there is even the question of whether God exists at all; and how are you supposed to find out anyway? What trust should we put in those documents that tell us about Jesus which we call the New Testament?

To all these questions, there can only be one reasonable response: come and see! Come and find out. Because the invitation of the Christian faith is the invitation to come and see and find God as he is revealed in Jesus. Jesus is God's way to God, and we encounter that story when we open the Bible.

In John's gospel, Jesus says, 'Whoever has seen me has seen the Father' (John 14:9). The letter to the Ephesians says that in Jesus we have access to God (Ephesians 2:18). These words of invitation, 'Come and see', are in fact the very words that Andrew said to his brother

Peter when he first encountered Jesus. We are invited to do the same. When we open the Bible and read the stories of the Christian faith, we can come and see Jesus. We can find out for ourselves if the claims of the Christian faith make sense. We can discover what the Bible is really about, what it really says and whether it can really be trusted. We can test it against our own experience. We can allow its challenges to confront our lives.

This will take time. When you open the Bible, you are not being invited just to read a book but to meet a person. The whole of the Bible centres upon the revelation of God in the person of Jesus Christ. The Old Testament points towards him and in the New Testament he is revealed as the one who is our God come down to earth. Therefore, this invitation – like the one that was given to Peter – is to a relationship with God, in and through Jesus. Because the Bible is the indispensible record of what God has done in Jesus, it is also the indispensable stepping stone into this relationship. But it is the relationship with God that matters. This doesn't mean we leave the Bible behind, just that it is not the Bible we worship. The Bible introduces us to Jesus; it then becomes the handbook of our Christian faith, guiding us through life until that great day when we will see God face to face.

This book offers a short introduction to the Bible, particularly the New Testament. What I have done is to arrange a series of Bible readings that tells the story of one disciple, Peter, and the story of what happened to him from his first being invited to 'come and see' through to his own witness to Jesus after the resurrection. He is the one whom Jesus himself described as 'the rock' upon which 'I will build my church' (Matthew 16:18). In this way, I hope that you will learn more about the Bible, be introduced to Jesus and begin to learn how to be a follower of Jesus.

Now, you might be thinking that such a person isn't really a very helpful guide for someone just starting out. But as you get to know Peter through the pages of this book, you will discover a very human, very frail, very fallible follower of Christ. Peter struggles, prevaricates, fails and soldiers on in the same way that so many of us do. In the end, he triumphs, not because of his brilliance or eloquence but because of his faithfulness to Jesus. Peter kept on coming back to see and find out more. If we do the same – and I pray that this book will help get you started – then we too can become disciples of Jesus Christ and, like Peter, be living stones in the church that Jesus built.

Introduction

This book is for new Christians who want to grow in their faith, and for more experienced Christians who want to reset the compass of their discipleship. It aims to help people:

- grow as followers of Jesus
- develop a love for the Bible
- understand more about the Bible
- establish a regular pattern for Bible reading
- allow the word of God to shape their lives.

It does this by telling the story of Peter, finding out how he became a disciple of Jesus and what it meant for his life, and relating this to the life of a disciple today.

In Peterborough Cathedral, where I worked for a number of years, there is a statue of Peter, depicting that moment when, having heard Jesus' call, he steps out of the boat to walk across the water. In the statue, Peter is portrayed with an almost child-like confidence – but he is about to sink. The story of his vocation is a story not just of responding to a call, but of learning what this call involves. He will have to be saved many times before he is able to become the person God is calling him to be. This book is about Peter's journey of faith, not because of Peter's brilliance or even his faithfulness, but because he shows us what being a disciple of Jesus is actually like.

Telling his story in this way will mean jumping around from one bit of the Bible to another. This is not necessarily the best way of reading the Bible, but will have the advantage of introducing different bits of the Bible. The Bible is not one book written by one person, but a vast library containing lots of books written over a long period of time by lots of different people. This book will give a flavour of the different gospels and the other books in the New Testament.

As we study Peter's story, I will say a little about how the gospels came to be written, the distinctive insights of one gospel compared to another, the different types of writing we find in the different books of the Bible and how they interact with each other. Each chapter also includes suggestions for further reflection and exploration, which will sometimes point us into the Old Testament.

How to use this book

There are 28 chapters in this book, arranged into four blocks of seven to be read over a four-week period. You don't have to read the book like this. You could just sit down and read it from cover to cover. But it is designed to be read a section at a time, one day at a time. This way, you can begin to establish a regular pattern for Bible reading, reflection and prayer.

Each chapter only takes about five minutes to read. At the end of each chapter there are suggestions for further thought, exploration and prayer. Don't feel obliged to follow up all the suggestions for further Bible reading, though this will enrich your experience of the book and help you to see the many connections in scripture, particularly between the Old and New Testaments. But make sure that, after reading each chapter, you do give a few minutes to reflection, thanksgiving and prayer.

A word on the authority of scripture

The New Testament has what you might call a 'derived' authority. Christ, not the Bible, is the 'Word of God'. The New Testament has authority because it is the indispensable body of evidence that tells us about the person of Jesus and the beginnings of Christianity. Its claims need to be investigated like any other ancient or historical document, but it stands up to examination. Indeed, the more we examine, it, the more remarkable it becomes, for in it we find the first-hand record of Jesus himself and letters written by Paul only ten or so years after the main events of the story. Therefore, because it is a collection of testimonies, stories, letters and recollections, it works like a compass rather than a map, pointing us to the one in whom authority resides, Jesus the Word of God. It is important to bear this in mind when reading this book and whenever we read the Bible. The people who wrote it were ordinary people like us. They had heard and experienced astonishing things, but always they direct our attention away from themselves, away from the written record to the source of what they are recording, Jesus himself.

Inspired by the Holy Spirit, who is always leading us into truth, the Bible is, for those of us who did not meet Jesus face to face in his earthly ministry, the way we can best meet him today. Through the Bible, Jesus speaks his words to us today. Therefore, as you read this book, I hope you will learn to love the Bible and be excited by its claims and challenges. But, more importantly, I hope you will be led closer to Jesus. The word was made flesh: we must not turn it back into a word. That would be a denial of all that the biblical writers set out to achieve. Rather, they want that word to be born in you.

Week One:

THE CALL

Andrew brings his brother to Jesus

The next day John again was standing with two of his disciples, and as he watched Jesus walk by, he exclaimed, 'Look, here is the Lamb of God!' The two disciples heard him say this, and they followed Jesus. When Jesus turned and saw them following, he said to them, 'What are you looking for?' They said to him, 'Rabbi' (which translated means Teacher), 'where are you staying?' He said to them, 'Come and see.' They came and saw where he was staying, and they remained with him that day. It was about four o'clock in the afternoon. One of the two who heard John speak and followed him was Andrew, Simon Peter's brother. He first found his brother Simon and said to him, 'We have found the Messiah' (which is translated Anointed). He brought Simon to Jesus, who looked at him and said, 'You are Simon son of John. You are to be called Cephas' (which is translated Peter).

JOHN 1:35–42

How did you first come to know Jesus? There are many different ways to faith. Some people are brought up in a Christian home and cannot remember a time when they didn't believe. For others, a religious upbringing stifled a faith that was then abandoned or rejected before something else happened to bring them back to the way. And, of course, most people today are brought up with little or no knowledge of the Christian faith.

But you are reading this book because something has brought you to the beginnings of Christian faith. For each one of us who is following in the way of Jesus, there are people and events that have helped us to come to know God.

For Peter, it was his brother Andrew. Andrew was already a follower of John the Baptist and so was on the lookout for what God was doing. The writers of the four gospels see John the Baptist as the forerunner of Jesus, the one who prepares the way.

The 'next day' referred to at the beginning of this reading means the day after the baptism of Jesus. This was the beginning of Jesus' ministry. Jesus came to the River Jordan to be baptised. This was very strange. John's baptism was for 'the forgiveness of sins' (Mark 1:4). Surely Jesus was the one person who didn't need forgiveness! Indeed, in Matthew's gospel, John says to Jesus that he should be baptised by him, not the other way round (Matthew 3:14–15).

In John's gospel, the account we are looking at today, John calls Jesus 'the Lamb of God'. This title is very significant. Its meaning is not obvious to 21st-century ears, but for those first followers of John, gathered at the River Jordan, and for Andrew when he again saw Jesus, it carried great weight, for the Old Testament often referred to the Lamb of God.

Hearing Jesus called 'the Lamb' reminded them of Abraham's words when he was asked by God to sacrifice his son Isaac. Abraham assured Isaac that 'God himself will provide the lamb for the offering' (Genesis 22:8), and because he was prepared to be faithful to God, even in this appalling duty, God spared the boy.

Hearing Jesus called 'the Lamb' reminded them of the sacrificial lambs that were offered each year at the Passover festival, solemnly remembering God's liberation of his people from slavery.

Hearing Jesus called 'the Lamb' reminded them of the gentle lamb led to the slaughter that the prophet Jeremiah talked about (Jeremiah 11:19).

Jesus is the one who does not need baptism because he is the Lamb of God who comes to bring forgiveness. Jesus is the one who chooses baptism because he is the suffering servant, the innocent lamb led to the slaughter. Through his baptism Jesus demonstrates his solidarity with all people. 'He became sin for us' is the striking phrase that Paul uses (2 Corinthians 5:21). Jesus comes and stands alongside the sinful, the wretched, the broken, the dispossessed and the lost. He says to Andrew, 'What are you looking for?' This is a crucial question for the human race. What are you looking for in life? Whom are you going to follow?

Following Jesus

You are reading this book because you have begun to follow Jesus. You have begun to find in Jesus the things you are looking for in life – assurance that in the midst of this wonderful and crazy world, you are loved; assurance that you are forgiven; knowledge of a purpose and a destiny to life beyond the things we see around us and yet immediately available to those who walk in the faith of Jesus Christ.

These things you are beginning to discover are the things Andrew discovered on the afternoon he spent with Jesus. He began to see life and faith and God in a new way, and what he found with Jesus that afternoon was so good that as soon as he got home he told his brother Simon all about it. 'We have found the Messiah,' he said. 'Messiah' is another word that we do not readily understand, but for Andrew and Simon, brought up in the Jewish faith, it meant everything. 'This person I have spent the afternoon with,' Andrew is saying, 'is the one chosen by God, the one our people have been waiting for throughout their history, the one who will usher in the reign of God on earth.'

So Andrew brings Simon to Jesus and the story of Simon's vocation begins. Jesus gives him a new name – and I shall say more about this another day. Let us pause here and reflect on how we have become travellers in the way of Christ.

For reflection and prayer

Give thanks: Who are the people who have helped you to discover and embrace the Christian faith? What has their witness meant to you?

Reflect: How can you be a witness to others?

Explore: Read these passages from the Bible that will take you deeper into the themes of today's passage.

- Isaiah 42:1–9: a description of the servant of the Lord, often referred to as the 'suffering servant' and, from the very earliest days of the church, always interpreted by Christians as a description of Jesus. It was meditation upon these passages from the Old Testament that helped the first Christians to understand the significance of Jesus' suffering and death.
- Revelation 22:1–7: a vision of the new creation in which the Lamb of God is seated upon the throne and is the source of light and life.

Pray: Jesus, thank you for calling me. Help me to follow you all the days of my life.

Jesus asks Peter to go fishing

Once while Jesus was standing beside the lake of Gennesaret, and the crowd was pressing in on him to hear the word of God, he saw two boats there at the shore of the lake; the fishermen had gone out of them and were washing their nets. He got into one of the boats, the one belonging to Simon, and asked him to put out a little way from the shore. Then he sat down and taught the crowds from the boat. When he had finished speaking, he said to Simon, 'Put out into the deep water and let down your nets for a catch.' Simon answered, 'Master; we have worked all night long but have caught nothing. Yet if you say so, I will let down the nets.' When they had done this, they caught so many fish that their nets were beginning to break. So they signalled to their partners in the other boat to come and help them. And they came and filled both boats, so that they began to sink. But when Simon Peter saw it, he fell down at Jesus' knees, saying, 'Go away from me, Lord, for I am a sinful man!' For he and all who were with him were amazed at the catch of fish that they had taken; and so also were James and John, sons of Zebedee, who were partners with Simon. Then Jesus said to Simon, 'Do not be afraid; from now on you will be catching people.' When they had brought their boats to shore, they left everything and followed him.

LUKE 5:1–11

We now pick up the story in Luke's gospel, though straight away it is a little confusing since we are reading about the same incident – the call of Peter – but the story is completely different. This can seem a bit of a problem for those beginning in the Christian way or looking at the Bible for the first time. How can both these stories be correct? Surely either Andrew brought his brother Simon to Jesus, and that was how it began, or this incident while fishing is the true account?

This is where we need to learn a little more about how the Bible carne to be written. As far as we know, Jesus himself did not write down anything during his ministry: certainly there is nothing remaining. Most of the people who followed him would not have been able to read or write anyway, and, even for those who could, recording things in those days was not the simple matter that it is today. People could not follow Jesus around, making notes of what he said or did.

All that we know about Jesus rests upon the memory of the first generation of Christians. This does not mean that the information is unreliable. Yes, people would have remembered things differently, and, because all human memory is selective, some people would have remembered some things in a particular way, according to their own interests and concerns. Certain features of Jesus' teaching, though – particularly his parables – would have been preserved as stories, pretty much the way Jesus told them. This is the way ancient cultures preserve and pass on their traditions and stories.

You can visit cultures today in certain parts of the world and witness this oral tradition at work. In some tribal cultures, still largely unaffected by western culture, the story of the tribe, its history, laws and legends, are faithfully passed on from one generation to another by word of mouth. This would have been normal for the culture of Jesus' day. There was a written culture for an educated elite and there was an oral culture. Almost all of Jesus' teaching, and the stories of what he did, would have been kept in this oral tradition. They seem to have been written down only when the generation with first-hand knowledge of Jesus began to die out and when the infant church wanted to order its life and witness.

There are actually quite a lot of accounts of the life of Jesus (called gospels), but in time the church gave authority to four of them. The gospel of Mark was, in all likelihood, the earliest, probably written within 40 or 50 years of the death of Jesus. Matthew and Luke were written later, based upon Mark (thus you will find that the basic order of events and many of the stories are identical) but adding in other material that had been gathered together. Then there is the gospel of John, coming from a different tradition and containing different material. Consequently, the exact nature of Peter's call is different in John than it is in Matthew, Mark and Luke (often called the synoptic gospels because they all have the same basic synopsis of the story). We cannot tell which is precisely right in saying how Peter first met Jesus, but both stories have important things to say to us about the life of faith and encounter with God, and both rest on the authentic collected memory of the early church. Rather than being put off by this inconsistency, I believe it opens up to us one of the great excitements of the Bible.

The Bible is the story of God's love for and involvement with his people, but it is written by the people themselves: it contains their own reflections upon the God who has inspired and redeemed them. It is not dictated by God. Therefore, when we read the Bible, we learn about God, but we also learn about what it means to be a follower of God and about how those followers in the past sought to make sense of their discipleship.

The pattern of calling

This story, shaped in its telling by many other stories in the Bible about how people were called by God, has four elements that are very striking and chime with our own experience of coming to know God.

- First, there is an awareness of God's presence. Jesus gets into Peter's boat and, pushing out a little from the shore, starts teaching the crowds.

  Can you remember your first awareness of God's presence in your life?

- Second, there is fear and apprehension. Peter, having been fishing all night and caught nothing, does not want to try again. Then, when this astonishing catch of fish is hauled aboard, Peter falls to his knees before Jesus and asks him to leave.

  Can you remember feeling unworthy of God's attention or love? Or frightened of what following him might mean? Or amazed by his actions in the world?

- Third, there is reassurance. The great catch of fish, however mystifying and fantastic, is a sign of God's generosity and sovereignty. Then Jesus says to Peter, 'Do not be afraid; from now on you will be catching people.' Jesus has a new purpose for Peter's life.

  Can you remember receiving a sign of reassurance, or coming to believe that God was commissioning you for something, that he had a new purpose for your life?

- Fourth, there is acceptance. Peter and his companions drop everything and follow Jesus.

  How much of this have you done? You are following Jesus, but how much are you still carrying with you that you need to put down?

This pattern of awareness of God, apprehension and fear, reassurance and acceptance is repeated throughout our lives as God's call is renewed in our lives and as we face up to the fresh challenges of being a disciple. In the rest of this book we will see what it means for Peter.

For reflection and prayer

Give thanks: How are you aware of the presence of God in your life?

Reflect: How can you discern the pattern of Peter's callng reflected in your life?

Explore: The following passages from the Bible are also stories about calling. Read them and see if you can discern the same pattern of awareness, apprehension, reassurance and acceptance.

- Exodus 3:1–12: the call of Moses.
- Isaiah 6:1–8: the call of Isaiah.
- Luke 1:26–28: the call of Mary.

Pray: Generous God, help me to face up to my apprehension and fear. Help me to accept your call.

Peter tries to walk on the water

Immediately he made the disciples get into the boat and go on ahead to the other side, while he dismissed the crowds. And after he had dismissed the crowds, he went up the mountain by himself to pray. When evening came, he was there alone, but by this time the boat, battered by the waves, was far from the land, for the wind was against them. And early in the morning he came walking towards them on the lake. But when the disciples saw him walking on the lake, they were terrified, saying, 'It is a ghost!' And they cried out in fear. But immediately Jesus spoke to them and said, 'Take heart, it is I; do not be afraid.'

Peter answered him, 'Lord, if it is you, command me to come to you on the water.' He said, 'Come.' So Peter got out of the boat, started walking on the water, and came towards Jesus. But when he noticed the strong wind, he became frightened, and beginning to sink, he cried out, 'Lord, save me!' Jesus immediately reached out his hand and caught him, saying to him, 'You of little faith, why did you doubt?' When they got into the boat, the wind ceased. And those in the boat worshipped him, saying, 'Truly you are the Son of God.'

MATTHEW 14:22–33

Now we are in Matthew's gospel. Over the next few days we are going to follow the gospel story as Matthew tells it. He was probably writing for a community of Jewish Christians. One of his particular concerns is to show that Jesus is the promised Messiah. This incredible story offers a kind of divine confirmation. Jesus' power over the stormy seas shows that he is the agent through whom God will renew the world, just as, at the very beginning of the Bible, in the story of the creation, God exercises control over the waters (Genesis 1:6–7). Jewish people hearing this story would have made such a connection.

So often, raging water represents chaos and danger. Indeed, the basic symbolism of baptism is drowning, not cleansing. We go down into the deep waters of death and we die with Christ. Then we are saved: we rise out of the waters to a new life. This is what happens to Peter in this story: Jesus saves him from drowning.

Before we get into the story, note how Jesus had gone off to pray on his own. Throughout his ministry Jesus is regularly putting aside time to be with God. He knows that he can't do anything without God's grace. This is the first painful lesson of vocation that Peter has to learn – to put God first, to act out of God's grace rather than his own strength.

The God who saves

The disciples are out in the boat and the storm is battering the boat and driving it from the land.

Early in the morning Jesus walks towards the boat across the water. The disciples are terrified, but Jesus speaks words of peace to them. First of all, he says, 'It is I.' Even these few words, like all the words in the Bible, and especially the words of Jesus, carry huge significance.

In the Old Testament, when God reveals himself to his chosen people, Israel, he reveals to them his name. We can read about this in the book of Exodus, where it describes the call of Moses (Exodus 3:1–14). Moses sees a burning bush, but the flames are not consuming it. God speaks to Moses and commissions him, but Moses wants to know the name of the God who is addressing him. God replies with a Hebrew word that is wonderfully difficult to translate. He says, 'I am who I am.' Another translation would be 'He who causes to be what is'. It is not that God is avoiding the question. Rather, he defines himself by using the verb 'to be'. God is saying, 'I am the one who is the source of all that is.'

Jesus uses a similar phrase, 'It is I', to describe himself. As we shall see, he uses similar phrases at other significant points in his ministry. He also says, 'Do not be afraid.' I have been reliably told, though I have not counted to check, that these words appear 365 times in the Bible. I like to think this is true. In other words, there is a 'Do not be afraid' for every day of the year!

Peter is doubtful, though. 'Lord, if it is you,' he says, 'command me to come to you on the water.'

'Come,' says Jesus.

Peter gets out of the boat, confident that it is the Lord and confident that in the Lord's strength he can walk on the water. But noticing the strong winds, and suddenly frightened, his confidence deserts him and he starts to sink.

This incident encapsulates some of the big issues about Peter's calling. On the outside he is bold and full of confidence, but on the inside he is holding back from putting his complete trust in God. Jesus trusts Peter and believes in Peter. He calls Peter to walk across the water and, when Peter walks in the strength of God's belief in him, he is able to defy the raging waters. But when he holds back, when he acts in his own strength, he sinks. 'Lord, save me,' he cries out. Over and over again Peter has to learn to trust the Lord and to cry out to the Lord. In our calling it will be the same. There are many storms raging about us. When we walk secure in the knowledge of God as the source of all that is – as the one who tells us over and over again not to be afraid, as the one who believes in us – then we will be able to navigate our way through the storms safely.

Like Peter, though, there will be many times when we fail and fall. When we are sinking, we need to cry out to God. Sometimes, people act so totally in their own strength that even when they are sinking, pride prevents them from asking for help.

In Chichester Cathedral there is a lovely stained-glass window that depicts this story. In the window, Peter is sinking beneath the waves and Jesus is reaching out to lift him up. Jesus' arms are very long and his hands are huge. It seems as if Peter is out of reach, but Jesus stretches out to hold him.

As we begin to discover what it means to be a follower of Jesus, we need to remember that there is nowhere so far away from God that he cannot reach out and save us if we call to him. You cannot hide from God, but you can stubbornly refuse to be found.

For reflection and prayer

Give thanks: How has God lifted you up and held you when you were sinking?

Reflect: In what areas of your life are you holding back from God and still acting in your own strength?

Explore: Read Psalm 89.
    The Psalms are like the hymn book of the Bible – a collection of poems and songs that describe almost all the emotions of being a follower of God.
    Psalm 89 is quite long. It tells of God's steadfast love and of his power in creation ('You rule the raging of the sea', v. 9). It also tells how the people of God reject God's ways, acting in their own strength. It ends with a plea that God will act again. We Christians believe that the longing of the Old Testament is fulfilled in the New.

Pray: Jesus, reach out to save me. Hold me when I am sinking, and take away my fear.

Peter declares his faith

Now when Jesus came into the district of Caesarea Philippi, he asked his disciples, 'Who do people say that the Son of Man is?' And they said, 'Some say John the Baptist, but others Elijah, and still others Jeremiah or one of the prophets.' He said to them, 'But who do you say that I am?' Simon Peter answered, 'You are the Messiah, the Son of the living God.' And Jesus answered him, 'Blessed are you, Simon son of Jonah! For flesh and blood has not revealed this to you, but my Father in heaven. And I tell you, you are Peter, and on this rock I will build my church, and the gates of Hades will not prevail against it. I will give you the keys of the kingdom of heaven, and whatever you bind on earth will be bound in heaven, and whatever you loose on earth will be loosed in heaven.'

MATTHEW 16:13–19

This exchange between Jesus and Peter is one of the great turning points of the gospel story.

Up until this point, the disciples do not really know who Jesus is. They have seen him do amazing things but they are slow to realise that he is the promised one from God. So Jesus asks them, 'Who do people say that the Son of Man is?' Notice that Jesus never tells them who he truly is. He usually speaks about himself using this strange little phrase, 'The Son of Man', which in many ways emphasises his ordinariness rather than his uniqueness. It is like saying, 'I am just another man, another son of Adam.'

The replies from the disciples show their uncertainty. They think that Jesus is like one of the great prophets. It is a bit like us today saying that Jesus is like Nelson Mandela – a great man, but still just a man.

Then Peter comes out with something astonishing. He says that Jesus is more than just a great man, greater even than the great prophets: Jesus is the Messiah, not just another Son of Man, but also the Son of the living God. Peter is the first person in the gospel story to make this connection. It is the faith connection. Jesus is more than just a great person: he is God come down to earth.

How did Peter make such a connection? Well, first of all we can note that it didn't happen all at once. He had been with Jesus a little while, observing what he said and did. It is still like this today. Some people come to faith suddenly and dramatically, but for most people it is a gradual process. People come into the presence of Jesus through the ministry of the church, and particularly through their contact with Christian people, and start considering the claims of the Christian faith. Then there comes a time when faith begins. This is either a moment when things click into place or a realisation that one's outlook on life has changed.

We can also note that the connection of faith is itself a gift from God. Jesus says, 'Flesh and blood has not revealed this to you, but my Father in heaven.' We cannot achieve belief through hard work or virtuous living or cleverness. Neither can our eloquence or goodness persuade others to believe. How some come to believe and others do not is itself a great mystery – but God does not force himself into people's lives. He comes alongside us, mysteriously and beautifully. We begin to consider what this might mean. Then come those moments of realisation and dawning faith, and even then we experience them not as something we have achieved, but as moments of enlightenment from God.

It is this that I am calling the 'faith connection' – a connection between our dawning knowledge of God and the gift of faith given by God himself.

The faith connection

Making this faith connection, as Peter quickly discovers, is not the end of a journey but a turning point – the beginning of a new journey. Peter begins the transition from being a disciple, one who follows Jesus, to being an apostle, one who is sent and commissioned by Jesus. This transition is symbolised by the new name that Jesus gives him. Matthew includes the story here to emphasise the new identity that comes from making this faith connection and beginning to live the Christian way. From now on, Simon is to be known as Peter, a name which means 'the rock'. Peter's calling is to be like a rock on which the new company of believers, the church, is to be built. You could argue that the nickname Jesus gives Simon is a bit rude. Jesus calls him Rocky. As we shall see, Peter doesn't seem to be much of a rock. Perhaps 'Sandy' would have been a better name.

Jesus tells a famous story about two houses, one built on rock, one on sand. The houses appear to be the same. It is only when the storms come and the houses are tested that we find out that one is useless: its foundations cannot hold and it collapses.

In many ways, Peter appears to be more like a house built on sand than a house built on rock. He promises much but he fails to deliver. He collapses when tested, just as he sank beneath the waves when he tried to walk across the water. But we shall also see that Peter becomes the rock. Gradually he learns to act in God's strength and to rely on God's providence. He learns to build his own life on the foundations of God and therefore to become that foundation for others.

For reflection and prayer

Give thanks: Thank God that the faith connection has been made in you.

Reflect: You may not have been given a new name, but in what sense are you forging a new identity as a Christian?

Explore: Look at the parable of the two houses in Matthew 7:24–27. It comes right at the end of Jesus' sermon on the mount. Jesus is saying, 'These are the foundations upon which you must build your life.'·

Pray: Loving God, build my foundation on Christ, recognising Jesus as Lord, becoming the person you call me to be.

Jesus rebukes Peter

From that time on, Jesus began to show his disciples that he must go to Jerusalem and undergo great suffering at the hands of the elders and chief priests and scribes, and be killed, and on the third day be raised. And Peter took him aside and began to rebuke him, saying, 'God forbid it, Lord! This must never happen to you.' But he turned and said to Peter, 'Get behind me, Satan! You are a stumbling-block to me; for you are setting your mind not on divine things but on human things.'

Then Jesus told his disciples, 'If any want to become my followers, let them deny themselves and take up their cross and follow me. For those who want to save their life will lose it, and those who lose their life for my sake will find it. For what will it profit them if they gain the whole world but forfeit their life? Or what will they give in return for their life?

MATTHEW 16:21–26

As soon as the faith connection has been made, Jesus is leading his disciples, and Peter in particular, deeper into the knowledge of God's ways. Peter realises that Jesus is the Messiah, but he doesn't know what sort of Messiah he is.

The Jewish people had been hoping for a messiah for hundreds of years, and at different times in their history this hope had taken different forms. In these days of Roman occupation, the hope was for someone who, at least, would be some sort of political and military leader who would vanquish the occupying forces and re-establish Israel as a force in the world.

Therefore, to hear Jesus speak about his suffering and dying cannot have made any sense to the disciples. Typically, it is Peter who jumps in first. He says to Jesus, 'God forbid it, Lord! This must never happen to you.' Peter means well. He wants to protect Jesus from the opposition that he is going to face. But this, says Jesus, is human thinking, not God's way. Peter has got to learn that the way of God is different. This is a lesson that all disciples have to learn. We want a God who will fit in easily with our ideas and prejudices. Therefore, without always realising it, we create God in our image. The hard thing is to be so open to God's will that we can be shaped in his image. This is what Jesus models so perfectly, because he is fully God and fully human, and this is what Peter is slowly learning.

Jesus is going to do battle with the forces of oppression and injustice and evil, but he is going to do it by love. He is going to absorb all the hate and spite that the world can throw at him, and he will go on loving, go on forgiving. In this sense the cross of Jesus will be like a lightning conductor, capturing and taking to itself and diffusing all that separates humanity from God. No, he will not be a messiah as many had imagined, establishing a new earthly kingdom. He is God himself, the Prince of Peace, restoring harmony to the world, ushering in a new creation. To oppose this work of restoration is to be like Satan.

Jesus goes even further. 'If you want to be my follower,' he says, 'then you too must deny yourself and take up the cross.' This will be the mark of those who walk in the way of Jesus – the mark of the cross – and those who follow in the way are required to learn humility and gentleness, to turn the other cheek and to go the second mile (Matthew 5:39, 41). It is by this radical loving that the world will be saved. 'For those who want to save their life will lose it, and those who lose their life for my sake will find it.'

We will see more about this next week when we consider the character of a Christian disciple. For today, there are two further points to make.

Take up the cross

Jesus says, 'Take up your cross.' How could he say such a thing at this point in the story? Did he know in advance that he was going to be crucified? If he did, how does that square with the claim that he is fully human, because human beings can't see into the future like this? And if he didn't say these words, if they were added into the text at a later date, what does this do for our confidence in the reliability of the Bible?

Jesus believed that his calling was to be the Lamb of God, the suffering servant, the one who would bring peace. He also knew that walking this way of suffering love would lead inevitably to opposition from the religious and political authorities of both Israel and Rome. He never avoided this conflict, and he sets before the human race stark choices about how we live and about how we love. Therefore he will almost certainly have set this choice before his disciples. He may not have used the specific language of the cross, since, as a full human being, he was unable to see into the future; but, as one so in tune with the will of God, he did not flinch from walking in the way of his calling. It could be that Jesus used the example of the most degrading kind of death in his culture; after all, crucifixion was a common occurrence. But it could be that as the disciples reflected on this witness in the light of the crucifixion, they used the language of the cross to bring out the full meaning of Jesus' words. Hence we can say that the Bible is true, faithfully recording everything Jesus said and did, while also acknowledging that it cannot be word for word retold as it happened. The later knowledge of Jesus' dying and rising informed the way the story was told.

'What profit will it be to gain the whole world but forfeit your life?' says Jesus. The temptation to 'gain the whole world' takes many forms, but here let us consider some of its religious manifestations – the temptation to be the holiest person who ever lived; to know everything there is to know about God; to believe that your way is the best way, the only way; to rubbish other people's beliefs; to gain the whole world of faith and belief and holiness but to forfeit your soul because you did not heed the words of Jesus to take up the cross and to make your life an offering of service to others.

For reflection and prayer

Give thanks: Jesus died for you!

Reflect: What will it mean for you to carry the cross? Where are the places in your life where you are called to go on loving even if it means opposition and suffering?

Explore: Have a look at Isaiah 52:13 – 53:12, another one of the 'suffering servant' passages that you may have read at the beginning of the week. It is likely that Jesus pondered long and hard on these passages and in them found a way of understanding his own calling. These passages can do the same for us, helping us to understand God's ways and make them our own.

Pray: Compassionate God, help me to take up the cross and to walk the way of enduring love.

The transfiguration

Six days later, Jesus took with him Peter and James and his brother John and led them up a high mountain, by themselves. And he was transfigured before them, and his face shone like the sun, and his clothes became dazzling white. Suddenly there appeared to them Moses and Elijah, talking with him. Then Peter said to Jesus, 'Lord, it is good for us to be here; if you wish, I will make three dwellings here, one for you, one for Moses, and one for Elijah.' While he was still speaking, suddenly a bright cloud overshadowed them, and from the cloud a voice said, 'This is my Son, the Beloved; with him I am well pleased; listen to him!' When the disciples heard this, they fell to the ground and were overcome by fear. But Jesus came and touched them, saying, 'Get up and do not be afraid.' And when they looked up, they saw no one except Jesus himself alone.
MATTHEW 17:1–8

Some years ago, a lovely old priest spoke to me about some of the experiences that had sustained him in his ministry over the years. He spoke about a few isolated incidents when suddenly, if only for a few moments, God seemed very clear and very close. It wasn't that he did not feel the presence of God every day. It was just that in those few moments God was so much closer, so much more real. He described these moments as his 'glimpses of glory'. Perhaps you have had a similar experience, but don't worry if you haven't. For most people, most of the time, our living the Christian faith is an act of will determined by our conviction about the reality of God and what he has done for us in Jesus. Only a few people have a constant sense of God's presence and love. (For many of us, there are long periods of barrenness when God seems distant and remote.) But there are also the glimpses of glory – those moments of intimacy with God that are different for every person and serve to sustain us through the times when faith is difficult. They are a foretaste of heaven.

It is this foretaste of heaven that happens on the mountain when Jesus is transfigured. His disciples see him as he truly is, not just a man (though fully human like us) but God sharing and glorifying humanity. The disciples also see Moses and Elijah with Jesus, representing the law and the prophets, again emphasising the point that Jesus is the one to whom the law and the prophets point.

The transfiguration is such a wonderful experience that, unsurprisingly, Peter suggests building tents so that they may stay on the mountain. But again he has got it wrong. The calling for Jesus, and for the disciples, is to come down the mountain and, sustained by the vision, persevere in the way of the cross.

The mistake that Peter makes is the classic religious one. He confuses the joy and intimacy that are sometimes experienced in worship with the promise of God himself. These experiences are not the journey's end, but the necessary rations to assist us on our way.

The four degrees of love

Bernard of Clairvaux, writing nearly 1,000 years ago, described the 'four degrees of love' as a way of understanding how we grow in intimacy with God and learn the meaning of Christian love.

- Love of self for self's sake.
- Love of God for self's sake.
- Love of God for God's sake.
- Love of self for God's sake.

The first stage is where so many people live their lives, self-centredly, concerned only with their own satisfaction and pleasure. Next is a stage that acknowledges the reality of God but is still only concerned with God in so far as our knowledge bolsters the self. This is where we create God in our own image and bolt on to our unchanged lives those few bits of religion that seem to suit us. The third stage – love of God for God's sake – is what we see happening to Peter on the mountain of transfiguration. It is the religious stage, and, sadly, many Christian people get stuck at it. It includes real love for God, but it has become completely separated from the needs of the world and, most damaging of all, it has lost all proper regard for the self that God has made and continues to cherish.

Love of self for God's sake is what it is all about – to love the life that God has given us but to live it to the glory of God and for the building of God's kingdom. This attitude to life is wonderfully expressed in Jesus' own summary of the law and the prophets, which is to 'love the Lord your God with all your heart, and with all your soul, and with all your mind... and to love your neighbour as yourself' (Matthew 22:37–39).

We are made in the image of God and we are very precious to him. That is why he has come to us in Jesus. The words that God speaks to Jesus at the transfiguration echo the words spoken at his baptism: 'This is my Son, the Beloved, with whom I am well pleased' (Matthew 3:17). These words, and this knowledge of God's unwavering love, were the driving energy of Jesus' life and ministry. 'Listen to him!' says God on the mountain. Listen to his words of love for you. They will shape and sustain your calling as a Christian, whether you have mighty religious experiences or not.

For reflection and prayer

Give thanks: Thank God for any glimpses of glory you have experienced.

Reflect: Are you in danger of becoming too religious, staying up the mountain and avoiding God's call to service in the world?

Explore: Read John 15:1–17, a beautiful meditation spoken by Jesus on the night before he died, which reflects on the intimate love and union between the Son and the Father, a union we are invited to share in because God loves us and has chosen us.

Pray: Loving God, help me to love myself and to give you glory by the way I live my life.

The calling of all Christians

Blessed be the God and Father of our Lord Jesus Christ! By his great mercy he has given us a new birth into a living hope through the resurrection of Jesus Christ from the dead, and into an inheritance that is imperishable, undefiled, and unfading, kept in heaven for you, who are being protected by the power of God through faith for a salvation ready to be revealed in the last time. In this you rejoice, even if now for a little while you have had to suffer various trials, so that the genuineness of your faith – being more precious than gold that, though perishable, is tested by fire – may be found to result in praise and glory and honour when Jesus Christ is revealed. Although you have not seen him, you love him; and even though you do not see him now, you believe in him and rejoice with an indescribable and glorious joy, for you are receiving the outcome of your faith, the salvation of your souls.

Concerning this salvation, the prophets who prophesied of the grace that was to be yours made careful search and inquiry, inquiring about the person or time that the Spirit of Christ within them indicated, when it testified in advance to the sufferings destined for Christ and the subsequent glory. It was revealed to them that they were serving not themselves but you, in regard to the things that have now been announced to you through those who brought you good news by the Holy Spirit sent from heaven – things into which angels long to look!

1 PETER 1:3–12

How can we even begin to describe the wonders and the benefits of our life in Christ? He has given us new birth into a living hope. This is our inheritance as Christians – imperishable, undefiled and kept for us in heaven, where Jesus has gone before us to prepare the way. We are the ones who have received blessings that even angels longed for!

Our calling is to rejoice and persevere in the knowledge and assurance of this truth – and it will change the way we live.

The implication of living by faith is one of the themes of the piece of scripture that we are looking at – a prayer from the beginning of the first letter of Peter. So far, we have only looked at passages from the gospels, but most of the books in the New Testament are letters, written to encourage and instruct the infant church as it grew.

This letter is said to have been written by Peter, but there is a problem here. First, the Greek in which the letter was originally written seems too accurate and fluent for a fisherman from Galilee. Second, its themes, particularly encouragement to non-Jewish Christians under persecution, reflect the concerns of the church in a period after Peter's death. (We don't know exactly when Peter was martyred, but it was probably in Rome under the persecutions of Nero in AD64.) Third, we know from other sources that it was not unusual in the ancient world for books and letters to be attributed to a particular person when in reality they came from the communities that the had person founded or was associated with, possibly resting on fragments of things they had written, or records of their teaching.

Towards the end of this letter, a follower, Silvanus, is mentioned, 'through whom I have written this short letter' (1 Peter 5:12). Perhaps first Silvanus, and then later scribes, have added to an original letter.

I say all this not to undermine your confidence in the Bible but again to be realistic about how such a library of writings came into existence and received authority. From the earliest times, this letter has been acknowledged by the church as communicating the authentic faith of the apostles. But in a world where many are only too keen to knock the Christian faith or cast doubts upon its historical basis, I think it is vitally important that new Christians are plainly introduced to the facts, as we understand them, about the Bible.

So what are we saying here? My view is that this letter rests upon the witness and teaching of Peter as it was communicated through the church, but was probably not written by Peter himself and certainly not in this form. This is true of other letters in the Bible, but by no means all of them. Certainly most of the letters of Paul were written by him. Indeed, some of them are the earliest records of the Christian faith that we have, predating even the gospels.

A good Bible will give you introductory notes about the different books and explain these issues. It is important to know about them for two reasons. First, they protect us from the false comfort of thinking that we can believe things without question, just because they are written in the Bible. (Therefore, we are better able to defend and proclaim our faith.) Second, we are led to the source of our assurance, which of course is not the Bible but Jesus himself, the one to whom the Bible always points.

Being the beloved of God

'Although you have not seen him, you love him,' says the first letter of Peter; 'and even though you do not see him now, you believe in him and rejoice with an indescribable and glorious joy, for you are receiving the outcome of your faith, the salvation of your souls.' These words, addressed to Christians who had not known Jesus during his earthly ministry, speak powerfully to us.

Calling begins with experiencing the call of God in our lives, the ever-circling pattern of awareness, apprehension, reassurance and accept-ance that leads us deeper and deeper into the knowledge of God's love as we learn the inexpressible beauty of the gospel, that we are the chosen, the beloved of God. Everything else – what we call Christian character, allowing Christ to be formed in us – follows from this.

We have seen this week how this calling was formed in Peter – the wonderful impetuosity of his dropping all to follow Christ; his slowness in accepting what this meant; his quicksilver realisation that Jesus is the Messiah; the vision of God's beauty on the mountain.

There is one lovely incident in Peter's journey that we have not looked at. After the story of the feeding of the five thousand in John's gospel, when people come back the next day looking for more free bread but end up disappointed, many leave off following Jesus. They find his teaching too challenging. Jesus then turns to his disciples and says, 'Do you wish to go away as well?' Peter replies, 'Lord, to whom can we go? You have the words of eternal life. We have come to believe that you are the Holy One of God' (John 6:67–69).

Being a follower of Jesus isn't always easy or pleasant: it makes hard demands, often brings us into conflict with the world and, in today's world, seems so out of step with most people. I guess that many of us don't necessarily want to be Christians but, like Peter, having caught a glimpse of the reality of God, there is no turning back.

For reflection and prayer

Give thanks: We have not seen; yet we believe.

Reflect: As you have started to read the Bible, which bits do you find the most inspiring and exciting?

Explore: Look at John chapter 6 – the feeding of the five thousand; Jesus' teaching that he is the bread of life, the one in whom hungers are satisfied; and how some decide to leave him.

Pray: Jesus, where else can we go? You alone have the words of eternal life; you alone are the Holy One of God.

Week Two:

SHAPING CHARACTER

Greatness

Then they came to Capernaum; and when he was in the house he asked them, 'What were you arguing about on the way?' But they were silent, for on the way they had argued with one another about who was the greatest. He sat down, called the twelve, and said to them, 'Whoever wants to be first must be last of all and servant of all.' Then he took a little child and put it among them; and taking it in his arms, he said to them, 'Whoever welcomes one such child in my name welcomes me, and whoever welcomes me welcomes not me but the one who sent me.'

MARK 9:33–37

We live in a society that exalts celebrity. Newspapers, websites and blogs are full of the latest gossip about the lives of pop stars and soap stars. The natural desire to do well and to do one's best is sometimes overtaken by the selfish desire to get on at the expense of others, to stand alone in the spotlight. Very few of us have not dreamed about wealth and riches and fame. Why else would so many lottery tickets be sold each week? Why else are quiz shows that offer huge financial rewards, or talent shows that offer 15 minutes of fame, so popular?

This desire to put self first is something we have already discussed. Christian calling is hard because it requires us to put God first. We still love ourselves, but we love ourselves for God's sake, and, in so doing, learn proper love and respect for everyone.

Building Christian character involves chiselling out those self-centred attitudes that harden the human heart. It usually takes a long time. To be exact, it takes a lifetime. But, by happy coincidence, that is exactly how much time each of us has got!

In this passage from Mark's gospel we find the disciples, Peter among them, arguing over who will be the greatest. They have been with Jesus for some time now and have seen his incredible effect in people's lives – his power to heal, his strength in facing opposition, his wisdom. They sense that he is the chosen one from God, and they start to dream of an earthly kingdom where he is the head. Now they wonder which of them will share this greatness. And Peter, no doubt, always a natural leader in the group, is probably advancing his claims.

Jesus comes alongside them. He knows what they are arguing about, but when he asks them to tell him they are shamed into silence. Jesus sits them down. 'Whoever wants to be first must be last of all and servant of all,' he says to them.

This is a hard saying. It goes against the grain of our desire to be important and well thought of and successful. We have to put others first. Our character will be marked by service.

Then he beckons a little child into their midst. 'Whoever welcomes one such child in my name welcomes me, and whoever welcomes me welcomes not me but the one who sent me.'

This is an incredible saying. Jesus says that in welcoming a little child we are welcoming him. Elsewhere he says that if we want to enter the kingdom of God, then we must become like little children (Mark 10:15).

Growing smaller

To live our lives as children means to let go of influence and power. It means to rediscover wonder and simplicity. It means to rediscover dependency. This also goes against the grain of the world. Aren't we supposed to be independent and grown-up?

While the world turns children into adults, Jesus is busy trying to turn adults back into children – children of a loving heavenly Father.

Christian character means getting smaller, not bigger; choosing the last place, not the first.

Many people confuse character and personality. Personality is something we are born with. It may grow and change over the years, but all of us have different personalities that are simply part of who we are. Character is something else. Character is created by the choices we make about how we live our lives. Christian character means to choose to be Christ-like in everything we think and say and do. It is not easy. Its first step involves letting go of the desire to be great.

For reflection and prayer

Give thanks: Thank God for the opportunities you have to serve others, however small they may be.

Reflect: What choices do you need to make in order to live your life with the attitude of a servant and with the heart of a child?

Explore: Read Galatians 5:22–26, a short passage about the fruit of the Spirit. As we invite Jesus to shape our character, so this fruit will be evident in our lives. 'You can tell a good tree by its fruit,' says Jesus (see Matthew 7:16–20).

Pray: Understanding God, help me to let go of ambition and pride. Help me to be your child.

Unity

> John said to him, 'Teacher, we saw someone casting out demons in your name, and we tried to stop him, because he was not following us.' But Jesus said, 'Do not stop him; for no one who does a deed of power in my name will be able soon afterward to speak evil of me. Whoever is not against us is for us.'
>
> MARK 9:38–39

From love of self for self's sake, we find here another example of love of God for God's sake. This time it is John getting it wrong, but we could easily imagine these words in Peter's mouth. Indeed, they may be words we have often said ourselves.

'He's not one of us.'

'Who does she think she is, saying or doing things like that?'

'I've been coming to this church for years. Who does that person think he is, telling me what to think?'

'They shouldn't be doing that; that's my job!'

'We tried to stop the person who was doing good, because he is not one of us,' says John.

Jesus asks us to relinquish control. The grace and power of God will work though many different channels. It is not for us to erect boundaries and barriers, saying which is legitimate and which is not.

There are many different branches to the Christian family – Anglican, Methodist, Roman Catholic, Baptist, Pentecostal and so on. As people come to faith, so they inevitably become part of one particular Christian church. The danger is that we see our bit of the church as being the only bit, or the best bit. We end up disparaging our Christian brothers and sisters in other parts of the church.

It is a great tragedy that the church is so divided. Jesus' prayer on the night before he died was that his church should be one (John 17:21). Sadly, this has hardly ever been the case. Christians have disagreed and fallen out with each other over all sorts of issues. Thankfully, in recent years, we have grown closer towards full communion through the recognition of each other's baptism, but the major branches of the Christian family are still a long way away from visible unity.

May they all be one

Jesus prayed for the church to be one, so that the world may believe. I reckon the world looks at the disunity and squabbling between Christians and concludes that if we cannot even agree among ourselves, what point is there in taking us seriously? If we cannot practise our gospel of reconciliation, we had better not preach it!

This failure of love and charity by Christian people is a tragedy that must break God's heart. I have often pondered on the words from John's gospel which say that after Jesus died on the cross, the soldiers came and found that not one bone of his body was broken (John 19:33–36). Since then, just about every bone of his body, the church, has been broken, and, through our failure to love each other, the world has been prevented from bearing the clear call of the gospel.

We must work to change this. If you are reading this book as a new Christian, resolve now to learn about and value your Christian brothers and sisters in other churches. Find out about them, worship with them from time to time and get involved in local initiatives where Christians meet and work together.

The Christian character is one of love and respect for all people. We should delight when we see good being done in the name of Jesus. Indeed, in multi-faith Britain we should delight in the good being done by anyone, and should work together with people from other faith communities on those issues where we can make common cause.

For reflection and prayer

Give thanks: Thank God for the good that is done by human beings regardless of their faith or denomination.

Reflect: How can you find out more about Christians in other churches, and what can you do to build unity?

Explore: Read John 17, the end of Jesus' prayer on the night before he died. Jesus prays for his disciples, for their unity and for their mission.

Pray: Generous God, heal the wounds of division in your church and help me to love my brothers and sisters.

Generosity

'Whoever is not against us is for us. For truly I tell you, whoever gives you a cup of water to drink because you bear the name of Christ will by no means lose the reward.'

MARK 9:40–41

These striking words of Jesus cut two ways. First, Jesus implies that if we follow him then we may be the ones who need to be given a cup of water. Bearing the name of Christ and trying to live Christ-like lives will mean hardship at times and will require sacrifice from us.

This is particularly hard in an affluent society like ours. The temptation is to allow the gospel to change some of our attitudes but to leave others unaffected. It has often been said that the last part of a human being to be converted is the wallet! If we bear the name of Christ, though, we must allow all of our life to be shaped by the values and standards of the gospel, and this will mean looking hard at the way we spend our money. Whether we like it or not, the way we spend our money speaks very eloquently of our priorities. To put it bluntly, if we spend more money each year on a daily newspaper, or on alcohol or evenings out or holidays, than on supporting the life of the church or supporting charities to alleviate suffering in the world, then very clearly those things take a higher priority in our lives than God.

This, then, is the second meaning of Jesus' words: we need to be the ones who are giving from the abundance of what we enjoy. In giving a cup of water to others, we give it to Christ, because Jesus is to be found in the poor and needy.

Building the kingdom

Generosity is not measured by how much we give, but by how much we have left after we have given. The poor widow in Mark 12:41–44 who, from her poverty, gave all that she had to live on contributed more than those who, from their abundance, gave a lot but also kept a lot back.

We also need to get involved in helping to build God's kingdom in the world, expressing our concern for the poor not just through giving money, but also in giving of our time and energy. One of the other reasons why people outside the church so often dismiss us is that they do not see our faith in action in our lives.

This again is a matter of character. Each one of us needs to make a conscious decision to be a person who is actively caring for the world, actively involved in making a difference and contributing in all sorts of ways to the advancement of God's kingdom.

The Bible is very clear about all this in both the Old and New Testaments. The prophets in the Old Testament rage against Israel, complaining again and again that the people worry about the finer points of religious observance while ignoring the plight of the oppressed and the poor.

In the New Testament, too, Jesus has a bias for the poor. The heroes of the gospels are not usually the disciples but the little ones on the edge of the story. They are Jesus' chosen ones – the ones who understand who he is and are faithful to his call. Peter blunders in and gets it wrong, following his own will, his character unchanged by the gospel. The little ones who know their need of God are true citizens of the kingdom. In fact, as we discussed in the chapter before last, they are the greatest in the kingdom of heaven. But they are great not because they are small or innocent but because their powerlessness gives them a freedom that adults usually lose. Children freely give whatever they have and share willingly, and they freely receive. We need to learn this same childlike attitude to life.

As our character is shaped by the gospel, there will be times when we are thirsty and, in our vulnerability, will need others to minister to us. This requires of us boldness to follow where Christ calls and humility to receive from others. Then there will be times when we are the ones who are called to give, and we must embrace this ministry with joy. It requires our money and our life.

For reflection and prayer

Give thanks: Thank God for the abundance we enjoy and the time and talents and resources we have been given.

Reflect: How is faith expressed in your life? How is your life a blessing to the people you know?

Explore: Read Isaiah chapter 58, a good example of God's righteous anger when the practice of religion gets separated from the pursuit of justice.

Pray: Bountiful God, give me a generous spirit, that I might share with others the riches I have received.

Faithfulness

'If any of you put a stumbling-block before one of these little ones who believe in me, it would be better for you if a great millstone were hung around your neck and you were thrown into the sea. If your hand causes you to stumble, cut it off; it is better for you to enter life maimed than to have two hands and to go to hell, to the unquenchable fire. And if your foot causes you to stumble, cut it off; it is better for you to enter life lame than to have two feet and to be thrown into hell. And if your eye causes you to stumble, tear it out; it is better for you to enter the kingdom of God with one eye than to have two eyes and to be thrown into hell, where their worm never dies, and the fire is never quenched.

MARK 9:42–49

We are still in Mark's gospel. The passages we are looking at this week follow on one from another, so the little ones to whom Jesus is refer-ring are still those little children that he placed before Peter and the disciples to show them who is greatest in the kingdom of heaven. But his warning to any who should be a stumbling-block to these children seems extremely harsh. Does Jesus really want us to hack off our hands and feet or tear out our eyes if they cause us to stumble or sin? I don't think we are meant to take this passage literally. Jesus often uses col-ourful and provocative language, deliberately exaggerating to make a point. But if we consider for a moment which parts of our anatomy are the ones that cause the most problems, and if we decided to cut them off, I wonder what would be amputated first. I think it would probably be the tongue, though some of you may be imagining other parts!

What Jesus' words do point to is a ruthless self-examination. We need to examine our lives in the light of the gospel and so shape our character. Notice, also, that Jesus identifies that the biggest problems are not what we do to ourselves but the way our actions (or lack of them) cause others to stumble.

Getting a faith lift

Here is a simple self-examination that you can use regularly to give yourself a spiritual health check. You can do this on your own and, in the light of your discoveries, ask God for forgiveness and seek to change the way you live. From time to time, though, and at least once or twice a year, it will be good to speak to your priest or minister, or to a trusted Christian friend, so that you can receive guidance and counsel. Sometimes it will be necessary and helpful to make a formal confession of sin – not because God cannot forgive you without this, but because it is good to bring our sins and failures into the light and to hear Jesus' liberating words of forgiveness spoken to us personally.

A simple self-examination

- Loving God: Have I loved God as I should, putting him before all things and seeking his will in all things?
- Loving others: Have I loved my neighbour as myself and given of myself to bring God's peace and love to others?
- Loving myself: Have I loved myself and lived my life in such a way that I reflect the love of Christ?
- Loving the world: Have I loved the world, seeking justice and safeguarding the harmony of creation?

As you ponder these questions, think of the things you could and should have done, as well as the times when you have gone wrong.

Sometimes the simplest definitions are the best. Sin is our failure to be like Christ. Forgiveness is Christ's assurance that he still loves us. Grace is the energy and blessing by which God can make us like Christ.

It is good for us to examine our life in the light of the gospel, for then we can open ourselves to receive forgiveness and grace. This takes character. So often, pride stands in the way of penitence. We make excuses for ourselves and fool ourselves into thinking that there is nothing that needs cutting out of our lives. We become like Peter, built on the sand of our own bravado rather than the rock of Christ.

So, consider what you have said or done that would be an embarrassment to Jesus. Consider the things you have failed to do that Jesus would have done. Know your need of forgiveness and experience the liberation that forgiveness brings. Then let your character be shaped by grace. You may not always believe in God, but God believes in you and is shaping you into the person he has created you to be.

For reflection and prayer

Give thanks: Jesus came to call sinners and to seek out the lost and lonely.

Reflect: The only thing that gets in the way of your relationship with God is your unrepented sin.

Explore: Read Luke chapter 15, which gives three wonderful stories about God's forgiveness – the parables of the lost sheep, the lost coin and the prodigal son.

Pray: Forgiving God, help me to be realistic about myself!

Wealth

Then Jesus looked around and said to his disciples, 'How hard it will be for those who have wealth to enter the kingdom of God!' And the disciples were perplexed at these words. But Jesus said to them again, 'Children, how hard it is to enter the kingdom of God! It is easier for a camel to go through the eye of a needle than for someone who is rich to enter the kingdom of God.' They were greatly astounded and said to one another, 'Then who can be saved?' Jesus looked at them and said, 'For mortals it is impossible, but not for God; for God all things are possible.'

Peter began to say to him, 'Look, we have left everything and followed you.' Jesus said, 'Truly I tell you, there is no one who has left house or brothers or sisters or mother or father or children or fields, for my sake and for the sake of the good news, who will not receive a hundredfold now in this age – houses, brothers and sisters, mothers and children, and fields, with persecutions – and in the age to come eternal life. But many who are first will be last, and the last will be first.'

MARK 10:23–31

Again Jesus warns his disciples against the danger of riches. How important it is in our society to heed this warning. Advertisements beguile us with images of what our lives could be like if we purchased this perfume or if we bought these clothes or drove that car. We soon start imagining that we need these things, and before long our lives are imprisoned by debt and desire.

Most societies give far too much regard to wealth. It is true of our society and it was true of Jesus' society. When the disciples heard these words, they were genuinely shocked. They probably believed that wealth was an indicator of God's favour and blessing. Now Jesus warns them that it is a snare that can prevent them from entering God's kingdom.

'Who, then, can be saved?' they respond.

'For mortals it is impossible,' says Jesus, 'but not for God; for God all things are possible.'

Here is the great promise of the Christian faith expressed again. Jesus uses the same words that the angel Gabriel used when he visited Mary and told her that she was to be the mother of the Lord. 'How can this be?' responded Mary. 'Nothing will be impossible with God,' said the angel (Luke 1:34, 37).

We do not need to work hard at achieving salvation through good works, generosity, sacrifice or goodness. All these things are important but they are not necessary for winning favour with God. It's not that God is unimpressed by our endeavours. They are just irrelevant. He is not a God who has to be won round or appeased or kept happy. In Jesus we discover that he is our loving Father. Therefore it is his good pleasure to offer salvation to everyone. Why? Because he loves us. Through the death and resurrection of Jesus, salvation is made available to the whole human race. In other words, our life in the kingdom of God is something we receive as a free gift, neither earned nor deserved. It is a simple consequence of being loved. Just as human parents lavish love upon their children, so God our loving Father lavishes his love on us.

Christian character works in the same way. It is not something we achieve but something we receive. By following our calling to be the beloved of God and by placing ourselves in right relationship with God, we receive the blessings that shape our characters so that we become like Christ. God gives us a new heart.

A new heart

There is a passage in the Old Testament that speaks about God putting new hearts in his people. It says that God will take away our hearts of stone and give us hearts of flesh instead (Ezekiel 36:26). This is not quite the exchange that some of us had in mind. We are all for having the heart of stone taken away, yet perhaps we would prefer it to be replaced by some super-bionic, pain-free heart. But what God promises is a heart of flesh. The new heart that God gives us will not be one that is immune from pain and suffering. On the contrary, we will feel more keenly the sufferings of the world. In following the way of the cross, we will venture more often into places of sadness and conflict and distress.

Of course it is Peter who butts in at this point, reminding Jesus that he and the rest of the disciples have themselves given up a great deal to follow him. 'This will be given back to you a hundredfold,' says Jesus. In the shared life of the new community of God we will enter family-like relationships, finding new brothers and sisters and parents and children. The church of Jesus is called to be this new community. The Christian faith is not just about the promise of a life to come; it is also the promise of a new life here and now.

It will not be without problems, though. 'There will be persecutions,' says Jesus. We will return to this theme in the next chapter – the way that Jesus leads us. Right now, let us rejoice that our salvation is possible because of what God has done in Christ.

For reflection and prayer

Give thanks: With God, all things are possible.

Reflect: Are you trying too hard in your Christian life? Do you need to relax and let God shape your values and concerns?

Explore: Read Ezekiel 36:24–28, a few verses that speak of God's great promise, a promise fulfilled in Christ.

Pray: Loving God, give me a new heart!

Service

James and John, the sons of Zebedee, came forward to him and said to him, 'Teacher, we want you to do for us whatever we ask of you.' And he said to them, 'What is it you want me to do for you?' And they said to him, 'Grant us to sit, one at your right hand and one at your left, in your glory.' But Jesus said to them, 'You do not know what you are asking. Are you able to drink the cup that I drink, or be baptised with the baptism that I am baptised with?' They replied, 'We are able.' Then Jesus said to them, 'The cup that I drink you will drink; and with the baptism with which I am baptised, you will be baptised; but to sit at my right hand or at my left is not mine to grant, but it is for those for whom it has been prepared.'

When the ten heard this, they began to be angry with James and John. So Jesus called them and said to them, 'You know that among the Gentiles those whom they recognise as their rulers lord it over them, and their great ones are tyrants over them. But it is not so among you; but whoever wishes to become great among you must be your servant, and whoever wishes to be first among you must be slave of all. For the Son of Man came not to be served but to serve, and to give his life a ransom for many.'

MARK 10:35–45

Here the desire for greatness again raises its head, and Jesus leads his disciples deeper into the mystery of his calling. The brothers James and John request places at Jesus' right and left hand in glory, but they have no idea what they are asking for, because the glory is not going to be the glory of a worldly kingdom. The glory of Jesus is going to be his death on the cross. It is on the cross that the true nature of God's love will be disclosed. Moreover, the places at his right and left hand are already reserved. Two criminals will hang with him when he comes into his glory.

'Are you able to drink the cup that I drink, or be baptised with the baptism that I am baptised with?' says Jesus. Even though the disciples say they can, it is unlikely that they understand the implication of Jesus' words. For us it is clearer, yet terrifyingly hard to put into practice. 'Can you drink the cup that I am going to drink?' means, 'Can you share in my suffering love for the world?' 'Will you be baptised with my baptism?' means, 'Will you submit completely to the Father's will and so direct your life completely by his purpose?' To be the beloved of God means to be directed by the will of God, to love the world with God's love, to serve the world with God's agenda.

Who can do these things? Not James or John; not Peter; not any of the disciples, although, as we shall see, after the resurrection they led lives of heroic witness. Only Jesus is completely faithful to the Father's will, and even Jesus, as we shall explore in the next section, struggles in Gethsemane to take the cup that the Father gives him. But through the Holy Spirit Jesus can work in us, enabling us to be centred more and more upon God. As this debate about who will be the greatest passes by, the other disciples (no doubt Peter among them, full of righteous indignation) argue with each other and chastise James and John. Again Jesus intervenes: 'Whoever wishes to become great among you must be your servant, and whoever wishes to be first among you must be slave of all. For the Son of Man came not to be served but to serve, and to give his life a ransom for many.'

Servants of God

The pattern of the Christian life must be one of service. Each of us must look for opportunities to be a servant, and this pattern of service should mark every aspect of our life, serving others in small and large ways. Whether at home or at work, we should be the person who is noted for going the second mile – making the tea, washing up, offering lifts. And if this means turning upside down the usual pecking order, then so be it. We are supposed to be ambassadors of a new humanity, and one of the best ways of modelling this is by disturbing those pre-conceptions that suppose that certain tasks belong to certain people. Make sure you are the one who is noted for never considering a task too menial to take on.

Every Christian should ask the question, 'How is my life a blessing and a service to those around me? How can I model the servanthood of Jesus in my daily life?' In answering this question, we shall travel a great distance towards becoming a true disciple of Jesus, for our character will be that of servant, one who puts the needs of others first.

The service of Jesus leads to the cross. There is no greater love than this. There is no greater service than this.

For reflection and prayer

Give thanks: Thank God for the opportunities that arise in daily life to serve others.

Reflect: When people think of you, do they think of someone who is eager to help? Is your life marked by service?

Explore: Read the parable of the two sons in Matthew 21:28–32 and ask yourself the question, 'What kind of a child of God am I?'

Pray: Jesus, teach me to be a servant.

Witness

Now who will harm you if you are eager to do what is good? But even if you do suffer for doing what is right, you are blessed. Do not fear what they fear, and do not be intimidated, but in your hearts sanctify Christ as Lord. Always be ready to make your defence to anyone who demands from you an account of the hope that is in you; yet do it with gentleness and reverence. Keep your conscience clear, so that, when you are maligned, those who abuse you for your good conduct in Christ may be put to shame. For it is better to suffer for doing good, if suffering should be God's will, than to suffer for doing evil.

1 PETER 3:13–17

One of the things that is hard for us to understand as 21st-century Christians, living in an affluent and comfortable society, is that first-century Christians expected to be persecuted. When you became a Christian in those days, you were doing something that was very likely to put your life in danger.

It is stirring and inspiring to read the lives of those Christians who did face persecution because of their faith and who carried on turning the other cheek and loving their enemy even when it meant their own death. In other parts of the world today, Christians face persecution. Sometimes, zeal for our own faith can too easily lead to hatred of someone else's. This affects people of all faiths and beliefs.

At the moment it seems unlikely that Christians in the west will have to face things like this, but the veneer of our civilisation is very thin. Evil still stalks our world, and there may be a day when giving a reason for the hope that we have means more than simply explaining to a bemused friend or relative why we go to church. Yes, we should bear witness to our faith in everyday life, but we also need to be aware of what other Christians face because of their faith, and what the cost of discipleship might be for us. Our readings in the next section look at the suffering of Jesus, when Peter fails to see what God is doing in these rapidly unfolding events. We need to be aware of our own blindness to God's purpose and how easy it is to hold back from the kind of witness that might bring us into conflict with the false gods of the world.

Facing persecution

Persecution and mockery and bearing witness in difficult and unfavourable circumstances are all character-forming. Most of us would prefer not to have to face them, but they will come our way in one form or another. If we overcome the temptation to run and hide, the other temptation (equally dangerous) is to start imagining what a great champion of the faith we have become, even a kind of modern martyr, riding the taunts and jibes of those who knock the Christian way.

The way to avoid both these temptations is to hold fast to the example of Jesus – to make his character our own. Make your defence of the faith 'with gentleness and reverence,' says the letter of Peter. This is very sound advice. 'Do not be intimidated, but in your hearts sanctify Christ as Lord.' Surely, this is the key to a Christian character – to sanctify Jesus in your heart, to place Jesus on the throne of your heart and let his peace reign within you. Then you will be able to speak gently and clearly about your faith whatever the circumstances, neither thinking too highly of yourself nor ducking the responsibility of bearing witness.

Placing Jesus on the throne of our heart is not something that happens only once in our lives, when we come to faith or when we are baptised or confirmed. It is a daily offering of our lives to God. Each day we need the transforming power of the gospel to shape and renew us. That is why a regular pattern for prayer and Bible reading is so helpful. It becomes the foundation upon which a Christian life is built. It is also a compass guiding us when we go astray. It is the daily challenge to become like Christ, the daily invitation to ask Christ into our lives.

For reflection and prayer

Give thanks: Jesus says that on the day when we have to bear witness the Holy Spirit will speak within us (Mark 13:11).

Reflect: How do you deal with persecution, be it the mockery of others or their apathy?

Explore: Read Romans chapter 12, another wonderful description of the Christian character, which ends with the exhortation to overcome evil with good and to do this by the steadfast witness of our love.

Pray: Jesus, fill me with your Spirit, so that I may live and speak and act like you.

Week Three:

THE WAY OF THE CROSS

Jesus washes Peter's feet

During supper Jesus, knowing that the Father had given all things into his hands, and that he had come from God and was going to God, got up from the table, took off his outer robe, and tied a towel around himself. Then he poured water into a basin and began to wash the disciples' feet and to wipe them with the towel that was tied around him. He came to Simon Peter, who said to him, 'Lord, are you going to wash my feet?' Jesus answered, 'You do not know now what I am doing, but later you will understand.' Peter said to him, 'You will never wash my feet.' Jesus answered, 'Unless I wash you, you have no share with me.' Simon Peter said to him, 'Lord, not my feet only but also my hands and my head!' Jesus said to him, 'One who has bathed does not need to wash, except for the feet, but is entirely clean. And you are clean, though not all of you.' For he knew who was to betray him; for this reason he said, 'Not all of you are clean.'

JOHN 13:2–11

In all probability, the last supper that Jesus had with his friends on the night before he died was a Passover meal. John's gospel sets the action a day earlier so that the death of Jesus happens at exactly the same time that the Passover lambs are being sacrificed in the temple. John is again making the point that Jesus is the true Lamb of God.

Whatever the precise timing of the meal, it is an occasion of great significance. The Passover festival is the time when the people of Israel remember God liberating them from slavery. At the supper, Jesus takes bread and wine and gives thanks to God. As he breaks the bread, he says it is his body. As he pours the wine, he says it is his blood. 'Do this to remember me,' he says (Luke 22:19).

After the resurrection, the disciples understood Jesus' strange words and actions at this final supper as a way of interpreting his death. Just as the bread was broken and the wine poured, so Jesus' body was broken on the cross and his blood spilled. Not only this, but Jesus had given them a way of celebrating his death and resurrection and receiving the fruits of his victory over sin and death. This remains the same today. The Eucharist (or Holy Communion, or Mass – it is called different things in different churches) is the main service in the Christian church. It is the service that Jesus has given us. Every time we receive Holy Communion, we are being nourished by his risen life. It is his service to us.

The company of love

John includes in his account of the last supper another astonishing story of Jesus giving service to his friends.

Jesus has a clear sense of his destiny. He knows that he is facing a showdown with the religious and political authorities. He is assured in his calling to be the Lamb of God. 'The Father had given all things into his hands… he had come from God and was going to God' is the way John puts it. Jesus is God's chosen one and this, clearly, is God's chosen hour. Therefore, when Jesus gets up from the table, surely it is in order that a throne may be placed in the centre of the room, that he may receive due homage from his followers? No. He takes off his outer robes, ties a towel around his waist and begins to wash their feet.

This is not the behaviour one expects from a leader, a master or a king, but it is really not so strange a thing for love to do. In this action Jesus reveals the overflowing generosity of a loving Father's heart. 'This is what God is like,' say the actions of Jesus, speaking louder than his words as he washes the feet of his friends – washes also the feet of the one who is about to betray him; and washes Peter's feet, although he knows that Peter will deny him. Indeed, when he gets round to Peter, Peter objects that Jesus is doing it at all. Everything seems the wrong way round to him: 'Lord, are you going to wash my feet?' Surely, if there is any foot-washing to be done, Peter thinks he ought to be doing it!

Jesus answers, 'You do not know now what I am doing, but later you will understand.' Peter is still learning the hard lesson of love – that God is revealed not in strength but in weakness, not in power but in service. 'You will never wash my feet!' he says.

'Unless I wash you, you have no share with me,' says Jesus.

The fellowship of Jesus is the fellowship of those who give and receive service. There are times when we need to be the ones prepared to wash the feet of others, but there are times when we need to allow someone else to wash our feet, and sometimes our pride makes it harder to receive service than to give it.

Before I was ordained, I worked for a year at St Christopher's Hospice, a place for those living with terminal illness. My first day on the ward was very challenging. I was frightened by what I encountered. I couldn't see people; I could see only illness, only impending death. A woman who was dying (in fact, she died later that day) called me over. She could see my fear and read my anxiety. 'Don't worry,' she said to me. 'Don't be afraid.' It was October and the leaves were beginning to fall from the trees. 'My life is fading like the leaves falling from the trees,' she said. 'But I believe in the spring.'

She ministered to me. I had arrived there thinking I would be the one doing the ministering, but I was the one who received – kindness and assurance.

For reflection and prayer

Give thanks: Thank God for the times you have received service from others.

Reflect: Whose feet would you least like to wash? By whom would you find it most difficult to have your feet washed?

Explore: Read some of the other accounts of the last supper: 1 Corinthians 11:17–33 and Luke 22:14–23.

Pray: Compassionate God, help me to give and receive service.

The new commandment

'I give you a new commandment, that you love one another. Just as I have loved you, you also should love one another. By this everyone will know that you are my disciples, if you have love for one another.'

Simon Peter said to him, 'Lord, where are you going?' Jesus answered, 'Where I am going, you cannot follow me now; but you will follow afterwards.' Peter said to him, 'Lord, why can I not follow you now? I will lay down my life for you.' Jesus answered, 'Will you lay down your life for me? Very truly, I tell you, before the cock crows, you will have denied me three times.

JOHN 13:34–38

These are virtually the last words Jesus says to his disciples before he dies. They sum up his whole mission. 'Love one another as I have loved you. I have shown you what true love is like. I have shown what real humanity is like, and in doing this I have shown you what God is like. Now people will know you are my disciples when you live your lives with the same compassionate love.'

Jesus says this after he has washed his disciples' feet. He doesn't just tell them the new commandment. He shows them what it looks like in action. He even washes Judas Iscariot's feet. Knowing that Judas is, in all likelihood, about to betray him, Jesus goes on loving him.

Judas then leaves to do what he feels he must do and there is foreboding in the air. The disciples are feeling confused and frightened. Peter (it is nearly always Peter) speaks up, but this time there is sadness and uncertainty in his words. 'Where are you going?' he asks. He knows that great and terrible things are happening, but he is far from understanding where they will lead and what they will mean. This is a path Jesus has to tread alone. He alone can do battle with the forces of sin and evil and death, for he alone is fully God and fully human. In his teaching, Jesus exhorted his disciples to show exemplary love: for example, he said, 'If anyone wants to… take your coat, give your cloak as well; and if anyone forces you to go one mile, go also the second mile' (Matthew 5:40–41). In the frailty of our human flesh, Jesus is going to walk the second mile of love. He is going to face the rage and spite of sin and he is going to keep on loving. This will be the ultimate demonstration of what it is to love. It will also be love's triumph.

The way of love

Peter persists, 'Lord, why can I not follow you now? I will lay down my life for you.' In Mark's gospel, Peter's words are stronger still. He says, 'Even though all become deserters, I will not' (Mark 14:29).

I am sure that when he spoke these words, Peter truly meant them. He really wanted to go with Jesus, just as he meant to walk across the water, just as he meant well when he wanted to build tents on the mountain top and when he rebuked Jesus for declaring that the Messiah was destined to suffer and die. But Peter's passion is flowing in the wrong direction. He wants to go with Jesus to protect him from those who would oppose him. He wants to go with Jesus so that he can shape events his way, even using force if necessary. His fiery temper, so easily roused, is incensed by the passion of Jesus, which is so different from his own.

Jesus allows himself to be handed over. Jesus does nothing to stop Judas, even though it is obvious that something is up, even though Judas as good as acknowledges that he is going to betray Jesus (John 13:27–30). 'You don't solve the problems of the world by turning the other cheek, by letting people walk all over you, by washing people's feet,' says Peter's logic. But this is the logic of the world, and when it comes to the crunch, this kind of logic will ride roughshod over anything in order to obtain its end – until, that is, it meets a stronger opposition. Then it will turn shamefaced away, because its concern is only for self: self-glory or self-preservation, but nothing in between, certainly nothing that truly loves another.

'Lay down your life for me?' Jesus replies. 'Before the cock crows, you will have denied me three times.' How these words must have stung Peter and how he must have recoiled from them, his anger boiling inside him. But these words show where misdirected passion leads. Peter has to confront the truth of them before he can go where Jesus leads.

It is the same for us. We have to confront our own ability to deny and betray Jesus. We have to be honest with ourselves about that vision for the world where we are at the centre. We needn't feel overwhelmed with guilt and shame when we face up to these truths about ourselves, for the way that Jesus leads is the way of love, and love does not keep a record of wrongs. It carries on believing and desiring, no matter what.

Our passion must become like Jesus', overflowing with love, able to absorb insult and suffering, directed to the glory of God, even if that glory is manifested in pain.

For reflection and prayer

Give thanks: For eyes to see where our passion is misdirected.

Reflect: Are you honest with yourself about your own capacity to deny and deceive?

Explore: Read 1 Corinthians 13 – Paul's great description of love's nature and purpose.

Pray: Jesus, help me to walk the second mile of love.

Gethsemane

They went to a place called Gethsemane; and he said to his disciples, 'Sit here while I pray.' He took with him Peter and James and John, and began to be distressed and agitated. And he said to them, 'I am deeply grieved, even to death; remain here, and keep awake.' And going a little farther, he threw himself on the ground and prayed that, if it were possible, the hour might pass from him. He said, 'Abba, Father, for you all things are possible; remove this cup from me; yet, not what I want, but what you want.' He came and found them sleeping; and he said to Peter, 'Simon, are you asleep? Could you not keep awake one hour? Keep awake and pray that you may not come into the time of trial; the spirit indeed is willing, but the flesh is weak.' And again he went away and prayed, saying the same words. And once more he came and found them sleeping, for their eyes were very heavy; and they did not know what to say to him. He came a third time and said to them, 'Are you still sleeping and taking your rest? Enough! The hour has come; the Son of Man is betrayed into the hands of sinners. Get up, let us be going. See, my betrayer is at hand.'

MARK 14:32–42

One of the great themes of John's gospel is the cosmic battle between light and darkness. Right at the very beginning of his gospel he describes Jesus as 'the true light, which enlightens everyone' (John 1:9). God's judgement is seen in people's love for darkness rather than light (John 3:19), and Jesus himself says in John's gospel, 'I am the light of the world. Whoever follows me will never walk in darkness but will have the light of life' (John 8:12).

In John's gospel, just after Judas leaves the upper room to betray Jesus, John says, 'It was night' (John 13:30). The suffering of Jesus happens in the dark. For a while, it seems that darkness has conquered.

Today's passage is from Mark's gospel. It is also in the night. Jesus leaves the upper room and goes to the garden of Gethsemane, where he prays. Jesus is aware of impending doom. It seems that God is setting before him a cup of suffering. 'If it is possible,' says Jesus, 'please take the cup away.'

These words of Jesus seem almost too human. Notice how he uses the word 'Abba' to address God, a word that would be best translated into English as 'Daddy'. Jesus speaks to God with striking intimacy, but the subject of his prayer is hard for us to fathom. We like God when he is almighty and all-knowing and all-powerful. We like Jesus when he is teaching and healing and blessing small children. Now there is anguish and pain. Jesus is very, very human in the garden of Gethsemane. He simply wants to know if there is another way of fulfilling God's will, a way that will not involve conflict and pain. He asks his friends to stay awake with him and support him through these hours of doubt and trial, but they all fall asleep. Quite alone, scared and tired, Jesus pleads with God: 'Father, for you all things are possible; remove this cup from me; yet, not what I want, but what you want.'

Jesus' calling to be the beloved of God and to show the true nature and capacity of love has led him to this hour. Who wouldn't be frightened, contemplating what lay around the corner? For Jesus is fully God, revealing God's great mercy and love, but fully human, suffering like us, suffering with us. His character has prepared him for this hour, but pain is always painful and nothing ever quite prepares anybody for the trials that have to be faced in life. His passion is in this sense to be passive, to allow himself to be handed over, to be the Lamb of God who suffers for the salvation of the world.

What do we make of the disciples in this story? They too are being very human. At Jesus' hour of need, when he longs for the support of his friends, they let him down, they fall asleep. The spirit is willing but the flesh is weak. In these hours of weakness and failure, Peter spirals into the darkness.

Tenacious loving

Most biblical scholars agree that the Passion narratives (the story of Jesus' last supper, arrest, trial and crucifixion) were the first bits of the gospels to be written down. They may well have existed independently from quite an early date before finding their way into the gospels as we know them. They were called Passion narratives because they revealed God's passionate love, his suffering in Jesus (the Latin root of the word 'passion' means 'to suffer') and also – the other meaning of the word – his passivity. Jesus shows us the capacity of love precisely through his refusal to run away or fight back or have the last word. It is his silence before his accusers, his forgiveness of those who persecute and beat him, his complete lack of hatred and his refusal to seek any other way that most reveal the true nature of God's unconditional love. 'Do your worst,' Jesus seems to say from the cross, 'and I will go on loving. Eventually, ultimately, in my dying and refusing to be beaten by your hate, you will be loved into submission and you will learn to love in return.'

Jesus' agonising prayer in the garden of Gethsemane reveals that this loving was never going to be easy. God chooses to let go of power and might, as we would understand them, in order to show the mighty power of love. And because his love is real love, then so is his suffering real. This is not a distant, disconnected God, but a God come down to earth, intimately, passionately involved in the world, ready to die for us.

We too need to hand ourselves over to God's will. We too will face agonising choices and times of trial. We too need to pray that we might follow God's will, not our own. Then we will come to the light of Christ, and be radiant with the light of love.

For reflection and prayer

Give thanks: Thank God for the humanity of Jesus, sharing our humanity, showing us true love.

Reflect: What are the ways in which you have preferred darkness to light and sought your own will before God's?

Explore: Read 1 John 1:7–17, words about the new commandment of love and about living in the light of Christ.

Pray: Jesus, be close to me when I face trial, temptation and pain. Help me to know God's will and then put it into action in my life.

Violence

Then Simon Peter, who had a sword, drew it, struck the high priest's slave, and cut off his right ear. The slave's name was Malchus. Jesus said to Peter, 'Put your sword back into its sheath. Am I not to drink the cup that the Father has given me?'

JOHN 18:10–11

We pick up the story in John's gospel. Judas has brought a detachment of soldiers to find Jesus, famously identifying him with a kiss. Jesus offers himself without resistance, but Peter is enraged. He has already declared his readiness to die for Jesus and now he fights to resist the arrest, though the odds are stacked against him. There is a kind of bravery here – there is certainly passion – but Peter has got it wrong. His instincts are all to do with self-preservation and violence. He lashes out with his sword but does not actually strike one of the soldiers. Instead he hits the high priest's slave, slicing off his ear.

John's gospel identifies this person as Malchus, a touching detail in a fast-moving narrative. Perhaps he is named because he was actually known to some of the first readers of this gospel. There are a couple of examples of 'minor' characters being named in this way in the gospels. The theory that this was because those people were known personally seems as plausible as any, and, if true, transports us back to the reality of the events being described. This is just how the disciples of Jesus remembered what happened, and their stories were faithfully passed down and recorded and finally gathered together into what we call gospels. Perhaps Malchus, who was once the high priest's slave, later became a member of the Christian community. We don't know this to be the case, but it is interesting to speculate!

This is another example of a place where the gospel accounts vary in the details they offer. Luke's account does not say that it is Peter who strikes out, and Jesus heals the ear of the high priest's slave, who is not named (see Luke 22:49–53). In John's gospel we are just left with the bloody futility of this mindless act of violence – a portent of what will happen to Jesus, a shocking reminder of how easily our passions are stirred to violence and an example of how one act of violence can so easily spiral into another.

These differences in the gospels are explained partly by the different emphases of the writers and the communities they were writing for and partly by the different information that the writers had to hand. We need to read the different accounts and place them alongside each other, seeing the different portraits of Jesus that they offer. We need not be troubled by the differences. They encourage us to look at Jesus from different angles. They help us to realise that no one picture of Jesus can ever tell us everything. Again, we are led from the words of the scripture to the living Word, who is Jesus himself.

Jesus' way is different from Peter's. His new commandment to love means loving enemies as well as friends. We should love our enemies, do good to those who hate us, bless those who curse us, pray for those who abuse us (Luke 6:27–28). 'If anyone strikes you on the cheek,' says Jesus, 'offer the other also!' (v. 29). In this way 'you will be children of the Most High… Be merciful, just as your Father is merciful' (vv. 35–36).

The model for this transforming love – this new way of dealing with each other – is God. God, says Jesus, is the merciful one, the loving one. Peter chooses the path of vengeance and violence. Jesus chooses the path of love.

The path of peace

In our lives there are many occasions when our instincts tell us to seek revenge, to exact retribution. Violence simmers just below the surface of the fragile equilibrium of our civilisation. Only when we have learned to love our enemies and to face the cost of turning the other cheek will we learn to be like God and let our passions be directed on to the path of love.

In the Old Testament we read again and again about a God who is vengeful and violent to his enemies. Of course we read these passages in the light of the revelation of God in Jesus, but it is wise to remember that it took an awfully long time for people to realise that God is not like this. Jesus' teaching was shocking to the religious people of his day, as it remains shocking to our world. In many ways, we quite like a vengeful God. This idea can justify our own vindictiveness and fury. It allows us to excuse so much violence. And we can still turn our back on oppression, still spend millions of pounds each year on ever more sophisticated weapons, still fail to embrace the radical love that Jesus shows us in his Passion.

'Am I not to drink the cup that the Father has given me?' says Jesus. He is ready now to receive the worst we have to offer. He is ready to drink the cup that the Father gives him. Perhaps, in Peter's wild act of violence, Jesus saw again the desperate need for the world to learn a better way.

For reflection and prayer

Give thanks: Thank God that Jesus shows us the way of non-violence and peace.

Reflect: How are you learning to deal with the violence and anger that bubble beneath the surface of your life?

Explore: Read Romans chapter 8, one of the loveliest passages in the New Testament, where Paul speaks not only of our new birth into Christ, describing us as adopted sons and daughters, but also of how the Spirit fortifies us in our weakness, giving us the spirit of Christ and enabling us to face difficulties, persecutions and suffering.

Pray: Merciful God, turn my heart from vindictiveness and violence. Help me seek the way of peace.

Denial

Then they seized him and led him away, bringing him into the high priest's house. But Peter was following at a distance. When they had kindled a fire in the middle of the courtyard and sat down together, Peter sat among them. Then a servant-girl, seeing him in the firelight, stared at him and said, 'This man also was with him.' But he denied it, saying, 'Woman, I do not know him.' A little later someone else, on seeing him, said, 'You also are one of them.' But Peter said, 'Man, I am not!' Then about an hour later yet another kept insisting, 'Surely this man also was with him; for he is a Galilean.' But Peter said, 'Man, I do not know what you are talking about!' At that moment, while he was still speaking, the cock crowed. The Lord turned and looked at Peter. Then Peter remembered the word of the Lord, how he had said to him, 'Before the cock crows today, you will deny me three times.' And he went out and wept bitterly.

LUKE 22:54–62

As Jesus is led away, Peter follows. He follows because of his love and loyalty. He follows, maybe, because he thinks he can do something – but he has already failed to help and he is hurt by these failings. What had seemed so exciting and so promising is now spiralling into disaster. Jesus had always surprised Peter, but now Peter is bewildered and frightened.

It is in just these circumstances of isolation and disappointment that it is so tempting to seize on an easy way out. So Peter probably gives it little thought when the servant girl first asks him, 'Are you one of them?'

'No!' he retorts, the words of denial easily tripping off his tongue. But in the next few moments he has time to reflect. He is in a tight spot. If they do find out who he is, what will happen? What will become of him? Will he be taken away like Jesus? Now, suddenly, the whole enterprise must seem foolish and futile. Why did he ever leave his fishing behind? Why did he ever follow this madcap preacher and put so much trust in this talk of a kingdom of justice and love?

This is how it happens – the next denial is even firmer: 'I am not one of them!' And the next firmer still: 'I don't even know who you're talking about!' In his final denial, Peter is not just saying that he is not a follower of Jesus. He claims that he has never heard of Jesus. His clinging to himself leaves him safe, but also leaves him utterly alone.

This is how sin operates. It divides and it isolates – one denial, one untruth, one little fiddle inexorably leading to another, weaving a web of deceit and falsehood. As we have already discussed, all sin begins with putting self first, with misplaced passion.

I remember, as a little boy, my mother, suspecting me of some untruth, would look me in the eye and declare that mothers could tell when little boys were fibbing, so please would I say again exactly what had happened. Under the scrutiny of her stare, I would crumple and admit to whatever misdeed I had been attempting to conceal. But, of course, as you get older you learn that your parents and, indeed, most people in the world are not able to read the reliability of your claims. It is quite possible to lie and cheat and steal and get away with it. Although most of us do not do this in major ways, we all construct our own little narratives where some things are kept carefully under wraps and others are shown in the light that will suit us best.

Judgement

God sees to the heart. He sees to the heart and he keeps on loving. He sees to the heart and his nature is mercy. When we become conscious of his gaze, we experience what the church calls judgement – not the weighing in the scales of our misdeeds as compared to our virtues, but the revealing of all our words and actions, our failures, omissions and fears in the light of his loving, penetrating gaze.

In Luke's gospel it says, 'The Lord turned and looked at Peter.' This verse is one of the saddest and most beautiful in the gospels, another massive turning point in Peter's journey – the time, perhaps, more than any other when he perceives the passionate longing of God for him, for poor, weak, lovely Peter. The Lord turned and looked at him. There is sadness at Peter's failure – Peter who, as ever, had promised so much – but there is continuing love. Jesus is calm where Peter is confused; Jesus is able to see Peter's wretchedness and isolation and he cannot stop loving him; and it is this love that is our only hope.

If it were a matter of running up a good credit balance of merit, we would all be lost. If it were even a matter of our worthy penitence, most of us would never make it. Rather, it is the knowledge of that steady look of love which is our hope of restoration. That look is Peter's judgement but also his opportunity, for the judge is none other than the merciful Lord Jesus.

Jesus looks at us. He sees us in a way we cannot see ourselves. He sees us, and our lives are brought into the light. He sees us, and we have an opportunity to turn again, to seek forgiveness and wholeness, to realise afresh the enormity of God's love – that he knows us, knows us through and through, and still loves us.

This incredible little sentence appears only in Luke's gospel, but it expresses a profound spiritual truth as we learn about God's passion for us, and also about his judgement.

For reflection and prayer

Give thanks: It is Jesus who judges you and he is all mercy and love.

Reflect: What are you foolishly trying to keep hidden from God? How can you allow all your life to be lived in his sight?

Explore: Read John 3:16–21, a passage about God's mercy and his judgement.

Pray: Jesus, I know you love me. Help me to live my life in the light and grace of your loving gaze.

Crucifixion

When they came to the place that is called The Skull, they crucified Jesus there with the criminals, one on his right and one on his left. Then Jesus said, 'Father, forgive them; for they do not know what they are doing.' And they cast lots to divide his clothing. And the people stood by, watching; but the leaders scoffed at him, saying, 'He saved others; let him save himself if he is the Messiah of God, his chosen one!' The soldiers also mocked him, coming up and offering him sour wine, and saying, 'If you are the King of the Jews, save yourself!' There was also an inscription over him, 'This is the King of the Jews.'

One of the criminals who were hanged there kept deriding him and saying, 'Are you not the Messiah? Save yourself and us!' But the other rebuked him, saying, 'Do you not fear God, since you are under the same sentence of condemnation? And we indeed have been condemned justly, for we are getting what we deserve for our deeds, but this man has done nothing wrong.' Then he said, 'Jesus, remember me when you come into your kingdom.' He replied, 'Truly I tell you, today you will be with me in Paradise.'

LUKE 23:33–43

All the gospels tell the story of the cross in a slightly different way and all are fascinating and worth comparing. In each gospel, what Jesus says from the cross is different.

Luke's gospel emphasises the tranquillity of Jesus as he goes to the cross. The cross is a triumph of love. Jesus shows great mercy: he forgives the soldiers who nail him there. Jesus is generous: he promises the thief who hangs alongside him an entrance to Paradise. It is as if Luke is saying that this is how it can be for us. If Jesus can forgive those who nailed him to the cross, he can forgive anyone. If Jesus can welcome into Paradise a common criminal who reaches out to him in the last moments of his life, then surely heaven is possible for everyone.

All the gospels stress the terrible suffering of the cross. It was a ghastly and sophisticated way of killing people, guaranteed to be long and painful. Thus the Passion of Jesus – his suffering and his love – shows how God shares the passion of the world.

The gospels speak of darkness coming over the land as Jesus dies on the cross, emphasising again the cosmic implications of what is happening. This is not just the death of a good and innocent man. Neither is it just about God sharing the suffering of the world. It is about God redeeming the world. Suffering will not cease as a result of the cross, but it can never be the same again, because God is in Jesus Christ, reconciling the world to himself, battling with the powers of sin, death and darkness, promising an eternal rest.

Thus the calmness of Jesus is in stark contrast to the failings and weakness of so many others. The religious leaders look only to protect their own position. The Roman governor, Pilate, just wants an easy way out. Judas has probably already hanged himself. The disciples are either in hiding or have fled. Peter is nowhere to be seen: he cannot face up to what has happened. Only a few of Jesus' followers, mainly the women in the group, make it to the foot of the cross. The crowd, who sang 'Hosanna' just days before, now bays for blood. It seems that what we are witnessing is the triumph of evil. But in the darkness and the sorrow of the cross, something else is happening.

The triumph of love

When I was a little boy, I often lost my temper, lashing out, getting into trouble. When this happened, my mother used to calm me down not by shouting at me or even punishing me (though I am sure some discipline was involved) but by holding me. She would meet my rage with a tenacious tranquillity. At first, this would cause the anger inside me to boil even more furiously, but soon I would find it melting away, the cool embrace of love taming and conquering the frenzy. Eventually there would be no rage left: not only was I loved, but I was loving in return.

This is how God deals with sin on the cross. He keeps on loving those who keep on hating. Jesus defeats sin and death by the resolute persistence of his love. In refusing to fight back, he refuses to give in to the misplaced passions that have led to this hour.

There is terrible risk in this love. If Jesus had given in to the taunts and indignity and sheer bloody awfulness of the pain, then love would have failed. It would have become less than love and less powerful than hate.

But Jesus is silent at his trial. He submits to the indignity and mockery as the soldiers dress him up as a puppet-king and lead him out to die. He does not resist. The few words that he does speak are words of consolation, encouragement and forgiveness. He is truly the Lamb of God. By allowing himself to be handed over to this suffering, and by fulfilling the vocation of love, God triumphs. He triumphs in the all-too-human flesh that Jesus now redeems. He risks the possibility of failure, as today he risks the possibility that we may never recognise the nature of his triumph – but that is the way it is with love. All it can do is to go on loving. It can never coerce and it can never wantonly hurt that which it loves. So Jesus has to die, and in his dying he shows us what living is all about.

For reflection and prayer

Give thanks: Jesus shares your suffering on the cross.

Reflect: Jesus died so that you can live. It is you he loves and it is for love of you that sin and death have been defeated.

Explore: Read 1 Corinthians 1:18 – 2:5, a lovely passage about the cross of Jesus and how it can appear as foolishness compared with the 'wisdom' of the world. There are lots of different ways of understanding the meaning of the cross. The Bible gives several different pictures to try to explain the great mystery of something that is really inexplicable. This passage in 1 Corinthians reminds us that it is a mistake to think we can ever completely work out the mystery, for God has revealed himself in a way that is deliberately weak and seemingly foolish to shame the wisdom and power of the world.

Pray: Jesus, thank you for loving me. Thank you for your death on the cross. Thank you for showing me what love is like.

The new life of Christ

Therefore prepare your minds for action; discipline yourselves; set all your hope on the grace that Jesus Christ will bring you when he is revealed. Like obedient children, do not be conformed to the desires that you formerly had in ignorance. Instead, as he who called you is holy, be holy yourselves in all your conduct; for it is written, 'You shall be holy, for I am holy.'

If you invoke as Father the one who judges all people impartially according to their deeds, live in reverent fear during the time of your exile. You know that you were ransomed from the futile ways inherited from your ancestors, not with perishable things like silver or gold, but with the precious blood of Christ, like that of a lamb without defect or blemish. He was destined before the foundation of the world, but was revealed at the end of the ages for your sake. Through him you have come to trust in God, who raised him from the dead and gave him glory, so that your faith and hope are set on God.

1 PETER 1:13–21

Another image that the Bible uses to describe the indescribable mystery of what Jesus did for us on the cross is that of 'ransom'. The word is used with reference to payment made for freeing slaves or prisoners of war, and the New Testament applies it to the work of Jesus. Our sins have separated us from God and it is as if we are in slavery because of them. Jesus pays for our redemption with his blood.

This image has its drawbacks, though. To whom is God paying the price? Is the cross really some cosmic bargain? If we take this idea too far, we lose sight of the great love of Jesus. When it comes to understanding the cross, we need to place the ideas of ransom and sacrifice, and sharing and loving, alongside each other. None of them can tell the whole story, but together they lead us into the trust in God that is spoken of in this reading.

The cross of Jesus shows us what love is like and what love can do. We can then become pupils in the school of love. And this is what the church is – a motley band of men and women who have caught a glimpse of God; lovers who are very much aware of their own needs and are learning how to love God and love each other.

The way we learn is by forging an ever-deeper relationship with God. This is where reading the Bible regularly, and reflecting on its meaning for our lives, can help so much. God's word speaks to us powerfully and personally, showing us Jesus and leading us into community with God. In this way we grow in holiness.

There are other ways, however, that are equally important.

Nourishing faith

You can't really be a Christian on your own. We all need the support and friendship and guidance of others. This is why it is so important to be part of a local Christian community.

Within the life of the Christian community, God has given us ways of being nourished in our faith. First there is baptism into the death and resurrection of Jesus, in which we have a share in his crucified and risen life and receive the fruits of his victory over death. This does not mean that we will not face suffering in our lives, nor that we shall avoid death, but it does mean that all our living and suffering and eventual dying are now set in the bigger context of Jesus' victory. Now we have nothing to fear, whatever life throws at us. We must pursue the way of love, trying to keep on loving, whatever happens to us.

This reading from Peter may originally have been written as a baptismal address to those about to become part of the church. They were being encouraged to persevere in the faith, to live holy lives. They were also probably being baptised in a church that was facing persecution. They had to be very serious about the commitment they were making. Fortunately, that is not the same for us today, but we need to be equally serious about the challenge of living out the radical love that Jesus shows us, whatever the consequences.

Then there is Holy Communion, the wonderful gift of Jesus' risen life, given to us in the form of bread and wine, but feeding us spiritually with his body and blood. We should really love Holy Communion more than we do, and be more thankful for this gift of life.

In John's gospel, when Jesus dies on the cross the soldiers pierce his side, just to check that he is dead (John 19:34). As they do this, blood and water flow from this heart. In later Christian thinking, these came to represent Communion and baptism, the two great signs of our resurrection life. These elements flowed from the dead Jesus on the cross. Even though our faith is rooted in his resurrection, it is the death of Jesus that is the great sign of the Father's love. The resurrection is the vindication of this love, the abiding sign of love's triumph. It gives us great hope – hope for the future and hope for today.

In the assurance of this hope, we find the energy we need for Christian living – a new heart, a new passion.

For reflection and prayer

Give thanks: Thank God for passion to live life well.

Reflect: What patterns of prayer, Bible reading and receiving Communion do you need to set in your life as you begin your Christian journey?

Explore: Read Ephesians 2:1–10, a passage about redemption and about discovering how to live passionately for Christ.

Pray: Generous God, help me to grow in faith and grow as part of Christ's body, the church.

Week Four:

ENDURING HOPE

The resurrection

Early on the first day of the week, while it was still dark, Mary Magdalene came to the tomb and saw that the stone had been removed from the tomb. So she ran and went to Simon Peter and the other disciple, the one whom Jesus loved, and said to them, 'They have taken the Lord out of the tomb, and we do not know where they have laid him.' Then Peter and the other disciple set out and went towards the tomb. The two were running together, but the other disciple outran Peter and reached the tomb first. He bent down to look in and saw the linen wrappings lying there, but he did not go in. Then Simon Peter came, following him, and went into the tomb. He saw the linen wrappings lying there, and the cloth that had been on Jesus' head, not lying with the linen wrappings but rolled up in a place by itself. Then the other disciple, who reached the tomb first, also went in, and he saw and believed; for as yet they did not understand the scripture, that he must rise from the dead. Then the disciples returned to their homes.

JOHN 20:1–10

The resurrection of Jesus is not immediately greeted with praise or wonder. First there is incredulity: where has the body been taken? Only very slowly do the disciples begin to realise what has happened. The story is told with as much disbelief as faith.

The first witness is Mary Magdalene. She comes to the tomb early and finds that the body of Jesus is not there. Seeing the stone rolled away, she probably thinks that the body has been stolen. She goes to tell the disciples, and Peter and John then come to the tomb.

The little details in John's account of this first Easter morning are fascinating. He tells us that John outruns Peter but doesn't go into the tomb. Peter, arriving second, does go in but does not understand what has happened. We can imagine him standing there, mystified by the stone rolled away, the emptiness of the tomb, and the linen that had wrapped Jesus' body lying there, with the cloth for his head folded neatly at one side. Emboldened by Peter, John then enters the tomb. He sees and he believes. Straight away he makes a faith connection. Somehow, in the emptiness of the tomb and the shocking absence of Jesus, John perceives his presence.

As yet, they had not understood the scripture that the Messiah must suffer and die, and that he would rise again. We need to remind ourselves here that by 'scripture' is meant what we call the Old Testament. One of the first tasks of the infant church would be to interpret afresh the prophecy and wisdom of the Old Testament in the light of the cross and resurrection, because now they see (or, at least, on this first Easter morning, John begins to see) that Jesus is the New Testament. He is the one who has created a new relationship with God, a relationship that fulfils and supersedes the old covenant that God had made with the people of Israel. Jesus is the new Adam, the new humanity; the new Moses, the new law-giver; the new David, the new king of Israel in a new kingdom that is open to all humanity.

It takes Peter a little longer to catch on to the new tune that God is playing, a song of joy and liberation to which the whole world can dance. On the evening of that first Easter day, when all the disciples except Thomas were gathered in the upper room and they suddenly found Jesus standing in their midst (John 20:19), I'm sure their first response must have been fear rather than joy. They had thought it was all over; now, with shock and disbelief, they realise that it is only just beginning. This strange story of resurrection that Mary had brought to them (for she had lingered in the garden after Peter and John's departure and had met the Lord) is true: the Lord is risen.

Seeing the risen Lord

What did the risen Lord look like? This is impossible to answer, but it is obviously a question that we must think about. All the resurrection stories speak of his being unrecognised at first. His appearance is not the same as in his earthly life. Partly, this may be because he wanted to draw from his disciples the response of faith, rather than coercing them into believing. Partly, it indicates a newness of life that is continuous with life on earth, but also different. In the morning, standing in the empty tomb, Peter is mystified and John has an inkling that something momentous has happened. After all, John had stood at the foot of the cross and seen Jesus' death. Peter had fled.

In the upper room, they see the risen Lord. They see the one who is now both a member of their group and also beyond them. He shows them his hands and side, making it clear that he is still the same Jesus, not a ghost, yet he appears miraculously in their midst. He is much more than a resuscitated corpse. He is alive with a transformed life.

He speaks to them his familiar words of peace, but then he commissions them: 'As the Father has sent me, so I send you' (John 20:21). There is work for them to do. They are to carry forward Jesus' ministry. They are the ones who are to continue his work of reconciliation and healing. They are to proclaim the rule of God.

What a turnaround! From the dispirited emptiness of Friday and Saturday, the great Easter promise bursts forth. To enable them to carry out this mission of love, Jesus breathes on them the gift of his Holy Spirit. Without this, the work will be impossible, but with the Spirit of Jesus working in them, they will do great things. They will have Jesus' authority to forgive sins, to heal and to make known the ways of God.

This Easter faith is as fresh today as it was on that first Easter morning. The Holy Spirit is as available today as on that first Easter evening. We may not see Jesus standing before us as Peter did that evening. We may feel more like John did in the morning, having to weigh up the evidence available and make our decision. But if we do decide for Jesus, he promises never to leave us and he promises that his Spirit will speak and act in our lives.

Jesus commissions us: 'As the Father sent me, so I am sending you.' Part of our growing as a disciple of Jesus is to discover what this means in our lives. It will vary according to our different personalities and passions. It will change as our circumstances change. But our vocation finds fruition as we become active in ministry, sharing the ministry of Jesus.

For reflection and prayer

Give thanks: The Lord is risen! This is the great truth on which the whole Christian faith rests.

Reflect: Have you begun to think about what it means to have a share in Christ's ministry?

Explore: Read John 20:11–23, the story of the first Easter day, carrying on from where today's reading ends.

Pray: Jesus, fill me with your Spirit and help me share in your ministry of love.

Breakfast on the beach

After these things Jesus showed himself again to the disciples by the Sea of Tiberias; and he showed himself in this way. Gathered there together were Simon Peter, Thomas called the Twin, Nathanael of Cana in Galilee, the sons of Zebedee, and two others of his disciples. Simon Peter said to them, 'I am going fishing.' They said to him, 'We will go with you.' They went out and got into the boat, but that night they caught nothing.

Just after daybreak, Jesus stood on the beach; but the disciples did not know that it was Jesus. Jesus said to them, 'Children, you have no fish, have you?' They answered him, 'No.' He said to them, 'Cast the net to the right side of the boat, and you will find some.' So they cast it, and now they were not able to haul it in because there were so many fish. That disciple whom Jesus loved said to Peter, 'It is the Lord!' When Simon Peter heard that it was the Lord, he put on some clothes, for he was naked, and jumped into the lake. But the other disciples came in the boat, dragging the net full of fish, for they were not far from the land, only about a hundred yards off.

When they had gone ashore, they saw a charcoal fire there, with fish on it, and bread. Jesus said to them, 'Bring some of the fish that you have just caught.' So Simon Peter went aboard and hauled the net ashore, full of large fish, a hundred and fifty-three of them; and though there were so many, the net was not torn. Jesus said to them, 'Come and have breakfast.' Now none of the disciples dared to ask him, 'Who are you?' because they knew it was the Lord. Jesus came and took the bread and gave it to them, and did the same with the fish. This was now the third time that Jesus appeared to the disciples after he was raised from the dead.

JOHN 21:1–14

This resurrection story echoes the story of Peter's call in Luke's gospel that we looked at earlier. Some commentators have wondered whether this is a single story that has changed in the telling and has found itself in two positions, serving two complementary purposes. We will never be sure about this, but John does use the story in a striking way, emphasising what we might designate the re-call of Peter; and then (we shall look at it in the next chapter) his very personal recommissioning.

The action takes place back in Galilee, and this is significant. Despite Jesus' momentous words in the upper room on the first Easter day, what has happened? Well, the disciples have all gone back to their old ways: they are fishing on the Sea of Galilee, almost as if nothing had happened. They have not yet found the new direction that their lives must take. As always, Peter has taken the lead. 'I am going fishing,' he says, and the others follow.

Just as in the story in Luke, they spend the night on the water, but catch nothing. At daybreak Jesus appears to them. At first (as in all the resurrection stories) he is not recognised. He tells them to try again, and this time there is an enormous catch, so large that they can hardly haul it in.

Jesus had told the disciples that when they became his followers, they would be catching people. The miraculous catch of fish anticipates the mission of the church, to draw all people into the household of God.

When Peter realises who is calling, he jumps into the water with characteristic impetuosity. He can't wait to be with Jesus. He gets to the shore first and the others follow in the boat, bringing in this astonishing catch. John even gives us the number of fish, 153, although there is probably no special significance to this. What is amazing is that the nets have not broken. So it will be with the church: all people are invited; all can be gathered in; there will always be room.

The church today needs to embody this vision of hospitality. All are welcome. No one has a special place, for all are special, all are firstborn sons and daughters. This is also a ministry that we personally need to embody (because together we are the church). Our lives need to be marked by gracious hospitality, always welcoming, always generous.

The company of the risen Christ

On the beach, Jesus has prepared breakfast. By now, all the disciples have realised who it is. They say nothing; they just sit down with Jesus. John then describes Jesus sharing the food in words reminiscent of the Eucharist, the service of sharing bread and wine that Jesus instituted at the last supper. These words, 'Jesus took bread, gave thanks, broke the bread, and shared it', would have been familiar to the first Christians reading John's gospel, as they are familiar to us.

The Eucharist (the word means 'thanksgiving') is at the heart of Christian worship. From the very beginning, the first Christians gathered to break bread together, remembering Jesus and experiencing his presence with them.

When we receive Holy Communion today, we are not just remembering what happened at the last supper, not just recalling Christ's sacrifice on the cross. There is a real sense in which we are sharing that breakfast on the beach, quietly coming into the Lord's presence and receiving from him. It is the risen Lord who invites us to his table; it is the bread from heaven that we share; it is the banquet of eternal life that Jesus spreads before us.

As I have said throughout this book, the Christian life is about a life lived in relationship with God. From this relationship our ministry flows. In fact, Christian ministry is best understood as the overflow of the love we have received. We sit and eat with Jesus and receive from him, and the love that is poured into our hearts spills over into the rest of our lives, enabling us to be true servants of the gospel.

In the book of Revelation, the last book in the Bible (and a difficult one to understand), there are some beautiful descriptions of this invitation to the life of heaven. The Lord speaks and says, 'I am standing at the door, knocking; if you hear my voice and open the door, I will come in to you and eat with you, and you with me' (Revelation 3:20).

For reflection and prayer

Give thanks: Thank God for communion with the risen Lord, especially for the service of Holy Communion.

Reflect: Is the love you receive overflowing into the rest of your life? What are the signs of this in your life?

Explore: Read 1 Corinthians 15, Paul's magnificent description of the resurrection, the foundation of our faith.

Pray: Bountiful God, thank you for feeding me with the bread of heaven and the cup of salvation. Help me to open wide the door of my heart, so that you will abide with me.

Do you love me?

When they had finished breakfast, Jesus said to Simon Peter, 'Simon son of John, do you love me more than these?' He said to him, 'Yes, Lord; you know that I love you.' Jesus said to him, 'Feed my lambs.' A second time he said to him, 'Simon son of John, do you love me?' He said to him, 'Yes, Lord; you know that I love you.' Jesus said to him, 'Tend my sheep.' He said to him the third time, 'Simon son of John, do you love me?' Peter felt hurt because he said to him the third time, 'Do you love me?' And he said to him, 'Lord, you know everything; you know that I love you.' Jesus said to him, 'Feed my sheep. Very truly, I tell you, when you were younger, you used to fasten your own belt and to go wherever you wished. But when you grow old, you will stretch out your hands, and someone else will fasten a belt around you and take you where you do not wish to go.' (He said this to indicate the kind of death by which he would glorify God.) After this he said to him, 'Follow me.'
JOHN 21:15–19

Here is a final reckoning for Peter – loyal, generous, impulsive and unreliable Peter.

'How many times should I forgive?' Peter once asked Jesus. 'As many as seven times?' (thinking this very generous). 'No,' replied Jesus, 'seventy-seven times' (Matthew 18:21–22). In this passage Peter learns the real meaning of repentance and forgiveness. He discovers how limitless God's love can be.

Breakfast is over and Jesus addresses him, beginning the conversation at the precise point of Peter's final failure. Hardest of all, Jesus addresses him as Simon. Jesus doesn't use his new name, the name he had given him; rather, he addresses him as the person he was before Jesus had met him. Such is the depth of Peter's falling. 'Simon son of John, do you love me more than these?' Jesus uses these words because Peter had promised at the last supper that he did love Jesus more than anyone. They might run away, said Peter, but he would not; he would stand firm, he would fight to the death.

In the Greek language in which the New Testament was written, there is more than one word for love. Different words denote different types of love. The word Jesus uses, *agape*, is the word to describe the self-less love that Jesus himself has made known to the world. It is the word used for the holy love of God. But in his reply (which looks in English to be the same word) Peter actually chooses another. He uses the word to describe the love one would express in human friend-ship – still love, but not that total, self-forgetful love which Peter has so obviously failed to exhibit. In that case, the exchange would be better translated as, 'Simon son of John, do you love me more than these?' 'Yes, Lord; you know that I am your friend.' For the moment, this is all that Peter can claim with integrity.

So Jesus asks again and slightly changes the question. He asks not 'Do you love me more than anyone?' (plainly Peter has failed in this regard) but 'Do you love me?' Again Peter repeats that he is the Lord's friend.

Jesus asks a third time. Not only does this poignantly recall Peter's three denials, but now Jesus adopts Peter's own word for love, not asking him, 'Do you love me with the same love that is of God?' but 'Do you love me as a friend?'

This third question, put in this particular way, cuts Peter to the quick. 'Lord, you know everything,' he replies; 'you know that I love you.' A better translation would be 'You see everything' – you see to the heart of me; you see my failures, my petulance, my pride, my fear; now see also my shame, my desperation, my longing for your friendship, my determination to be the person you have called me to become.

Feed my sheep

With each reply comes a commission – first to feed the lambs, the little ones of the flock; then to tend the sheep, to give the flock some general guidance. Finally, because Jesus does indeed see to the heart and see who Peter is and who he can become, he says, 'Feed my sheep' – become the one who will supply the needs of my people; be again the rock on which I build my church.

Jesus' choice of these words echoes his own calling. Jesus is the good shepherd who calls his sheep by name and knows them, who is prepared to lay down his life for them (John 10:4, 11). Now Peter's life must be directed by his calling to be the one on whom Christ is building his church. Now he will find the strength and resources to be the rock. Now he will be restored. This will not make his life easy, because he will have to face the trials that hitherto he has avoided, but now he will truly follow Jesus. This is the meaning of Jesus' words as he resets the compass of Peter's life: '"Very truly, I tell you, when you were younger, you used to fasten your own belt and go wherever you wished. But when you grow old, you will stretch out your hands, and someone else will fasten a belt around you and take you where you do not wish to go." (He said this to indicate the kind of death by which he would glorify God.) … "Follow me."'

Likewise, Jesus can reset the compass of our lives.

A few days earlier, at the last supper, Jesus had said, 'Where I am going, you cannot follow' (John 13:36). Now he says, 'Follow me.' Now it is possible – possible for Peter and possible for all humanity. Jesus has won the victory over sin and death, the Holy Spirit is available to all, and if someone as reckless and cowardly as Peter can follow, then there is hope for everyone.

For reflection and prayer

Give thanks: Jesus sees, forgives, restores, commissions.

Reflect: How is Jesus commissioning you? What is your ministry to be?

Explore: Read Psalm 63, a song that cries out to God, almost like a teenage love song. Is this what Jesus saw in Peter, despite his failings – this great longing for God? After all, Peter himself had said that there was nowhere else to go (John 6:68). Does God see this same longing in us?

Pray: Jesus, help me to love you with the same holy love with which you have loved me.

Peter heals

One day Peter and John were going up to the temple at the hour of prayer, at three o'clock in the afternoon. And a man lame from birth was being carried in. People would lay him daily at the gate of the temple called the Beautiful Gate so that he could ask for alms from those entering the temple. When he saw Peter and John about to go into the temple, he asked them for alms. Peter looked intently at him, as did John, and said, 'Look at us.' And he fixed his attention on them, expecting to receive something from them. But Peter said, 'I have no silver or gold, but what I have I give you; in the name of Jesus Christ of Nazareth, stand up and walk.' And he took him by the right hand and raised him up; and immediately his feet and ankles were made strong. Jumping up, he stood and began to walk, and he entered the temple with them, walking and leaping and praising God. All the people saw him walking and praising God, and they recognised him as the one who used to sit and ask for alms at the Beautiful Gate of the temple; and they were filled with wonder and amazement at what had happened to him.

ACTS 3:1–10

We are now in the Acts of the Apostles, the book in the New Testament that tells the story of the early church. A better name might be the Acts of the Holy Spirit. It is written by Luke and is a kind of Part Two to his gospel (notice how both Luke's gospel and Acts begin with mention of a man named Theophilus, the person to whom Luke is writing his account). The story picks up where the gospels end, with Jesus ascending to the Father. The disciples are confused and uncertain what to do next. Then comes the great day of Pentecost and, with the coming of the Holy Spirit, the disciples discover energy, eloquence and passion. They discover that they have a share in Christ's ministry (Acts 2:1–4). Their lives are transformed and redirected. It is an incredible story. The Holy Spirit leads, cajoles and inspires the apostles to take the good news of God's love in Christ to the entire world.

This same Holy Spirit is available to us today. It is the Holy Spirit who brings the Bible to life when we read it, enabling the word of God to speak to us personally and directly. It is the Holy Spirit who inspires us to lift up our voices in praise of God. It is the Holy Spirit who transforms us into the likeness of Christ. It is the Spirit of Jesus, breathed on the disciples and poured afresh into the hearts of believers in every age, who enables us to be the children of God and to discover how we might share God's ministry in the world. The Acts of the Apostles is, if you like, the only book of the Bible yet to be finished, because the Holy Spirit is urging us today to take part in the apostolic work of sharing the gospel and building the kingdom.

Peter and John's healing of the cripple who begged for alms at the Beautiful Gate is the first sign that the power of Jesus is now entrusted to his church. To get the real flavour and impact of this story, it is worth reading the two chapters that come before it. They tell the story of the ascension, the coming of the Holy Spirit, Peter preaching to the crowds and the common life of the disciples as they gather together, a transformed community, to break bread together and praise God.

Now, though, we see Peter transformed. No longer is he acting in his own strength, but he is trusting completely in the strength of God. 'I have no silver or gold,' says Peter, 'but what I have I give you; in the name of Jesus Christ of Nazareth, stand up and walk.' With these words we see that Peter has become the rock, the steadfast foundation upon which the church can be built, and this is so because Peter is now so firmly built on Christ. He takes the crippled man by the right hand and raises him up. Immediately the man's feet and ankles are made strong. He jumps up and begins to walk. He dances into the temple, leaping and praising God.

The people are amazed, and, if we read on a bit, we find that some of them cling to Peter and John, imagining that they have miraculous powers. But Peter is no longer interested in receiving any glory for himself. Nor is he troubled by facing the crowd, or even having to cope with their mockery or disappointment. He speaks to them boldly: 'Why do you stare at us, as though by our own power or piety we had made him walk?' (Acts 3:12). It is God who has done this, says Peter, whose servant Jesus you rejected and killed and whom God has raised from the dead: 'The faith that is through Jesus has given him this perfect health' (Acts 3:16).

The power that Peter displays is all from God. Peter has discovered his purpose and his ministry. Through the Holy Spirit, that power is available to all. It is the power of the risen Christ.

The power of love

We need to be careful about how we use the word 'power'. It can so easily be interpreted in unhelpful, worldly ways, conjuring up images of might and domination. The power that we speak of is the power of Jesus. It is the power to go on loving to the point of death. It is the power that longs to bring healing and wholeness to all people. It is the power of love and therefore it can never coerce or manipulate.

Peter is merely the channel of this great love, and he had to be broken so that God could use him. It will be the same for us. We will be challenged and changed by our growing relationship with God. Through the Holy Spirit we can discover our purpose and our ministry. With Peter we can acknowledge our poverty in the things the world would count important and valuable, offering instead the inestimable riches of Christ, who alone can heal and save.

For reflection and prayer

Give thanks: Thank God for the gift of the Holy Spirit who forms Christ in us.

Reflect: Do you pray to receive the gifts of the Spirit, asking the Holy Spirit to guide and direct your life?

Explore: Read the first three chapters of the Acts of the Apostles. They give a wonderful, dramatic account of the birth of the church and the transforming work of the Spirit.

Pray: All-powerful God, show me the might of your love and make me a channel of your peace.

Peter witnessing

While Peter and John were speaking to the people, the priests, the captain of the temple, and the Sadducees came to them, much annoyed because they were teaching the people and proclaiming that in Jesus there is the resurrection of the dead. So they arrested them and put them in custody until the next day, for it was already evening. But many of those who heard the word believed; and they numbered about five thousand.

The next day their rulers, elders and scribes assembled in Jerusalem, with Annas the high priest, Caiaphas, John, and Alexander, and all who were of the high-priestly family. When they had made the prisoners stand in their midst, they inquired, 'By what power or by what name did you do this?' Then Peter, filled with the Holy Spirit, said to them, 'Rulers of the people and elders, if we are questioned today because of a good deed done to someone who was sick and are asked how this man has been healed, let it be known to all of you, and to all the people of Israel, that this man is standing before you in good health by the name of Jesus Christ of Nazareth, whom you crucified, whom God raised from the dead. This Jesus is "the stone that was rejected by you, the builders; has become the cornerstone." There is salvation in no one else, for there is no other name under heaven given among mortals by which we must be saved.'

Now when they saw the boldness of Peter and John and realised that they were uneducated and ordinary men, they were amazed and recognised them as companions of Jesus. When they saw the man who had been cured standing beside them, they had nothing to say in opposition. So they ordered them to leave the council while they discussed the matter with one another. They said, 'What will we do with them? For it is obvious to all who live in Jerusalem that a notable sign has been done through them; we cannot deny it. But to keep it from spreading further among the people, let us warn them to speak no more to anyone in this name.' So they called them and ordered them not to speak or teach at all in the name of Jesus. But Peter and John answered them, 'Whether it is right in God's sight to listen to you rather than to God, you must judge; for we cannot keep from speaking about what we have seen and heard.'

ACTS 4:1–20

In this passage we begin to see the irresistible charm and power of the gospel. Peter and John are thrown in prison because they carry on speaking about Jesus and teaching about the resurrection, but their witness carries conviction and 5000 people come to believe.

The next day, the religious leaders question them about the crippled man they had healed, and in the same straightforward language with which they had healed the man himself, they bear witness to Jesus. 'There is salvation in no one else,' they say, 'for there is no other name under heaven... by which we must be saved.'

The message of the gospel is really very simple. Jesus is God's Son, his chosen one. He was crucified and God has raised him to life, and this new resurrection life is available to all people through the gift of the Holy Spirit. A new relationship with God is now possible, and healing and salvation are available to all.

All the disciples do is simply tell this story of God's love and mercy wherever they go. Because it is the risen Lord himself who has entrusted the message to them, they have no fear. In fact, one of the best proofs of the resurrection is the spread of the gospel across much of the world in such a very short time. There is plenty of evidence to show how this happened, and yet we know that it began with a few peasant fishermen – Peter and the other disciples. How else can we account for the amazing turnaround of their lives? How else would they have achieved this astonishing mission, unless they had seen Jesus raised from the dead and had been empowered by the Holy Spirit? Indeed, why else would they do such a thing – giving their lives for this gospel – unless they had experienced its truth and grace?

In this passage we also sense the exasperation of the religious leaders. They see the boldness of Peter and John standing before them – uneducated, ordinary men – and they are amazed. They also see the man who has been cured standing beside them and they cannot doubt the evidence of their own eyes. They are flabbergasted and can say nothing in opposition. It is obvious that something incredible has happened.

As a last resort, they instruct Peter and John to say nothing more about Jesus, but even this fails. 'We cannot keep from speaking about what we have seen and heard,' they reply.

Becoming witnesses

Of course, many of us today do not feel quite like Peter and John. In fact, we may feel very reluctant to say anything about our faith. Here are some ways forward.

- First of all, be firmly rooted in the faith itself. You are built on the solid rock of what God has done in Jesus. The stone rejected, cast away and crucified has become the cornerstone: God has raised Jesus from death and therefore all of life is transformed. There is no longer any need to fear. It won't always feel like this, and there will be times when doubts and anxiety crowd in, but believing must often be an act of will. We commit ourselves to the Christian way, basing our faith on what God has done in Christ, rather than on how we feel about it at the time.

- Second, begin to look for ways to share faith with others. Sometimes those closest to us are the hardest to speak to about matters of faith. Perhaps you will start with a colleague at work or another acquaintance, but once you start looking, it is amazing how many small opportunities there are to say something about the Christian way.

- Live your faith. The best advertisement for the Christian faith is a Christian life! Have a hunger and thirst for God's kingdom, and become a sign of that kingdom yourself.

- Begin praying for people you know – this is a ministry to which we are all called – and pray that, when opportunities do arise, you can make the best of them.

- Think about your own faith story – the people and events that brought you into the fellowship of Christ. Learn to love this story, your story of how you have come to know Jesus. There is something irresistible and fascinating about people's stories and it will be your best resource in sharing the faith. All that Peter and John did was to tell it how it was. They recounted their experience. This will be our ministry as well.

Over many centuries, as the church reflected on the amazing experiences of the first disciples, so the doctrines and formularies of the Christian faith set out the boundaries of our faith. But it all started as experience.

As the disciples shared their experience and as people questioned them, so they came to understand more of the significance, implications and inner meaning of what had happened. This process still goes on. As we share the story of Jesus and the story of our own faith, so we will come to understand more of what we believe and so we will come to discover more of God's purpose for our lives.

For reflection and prayer

Give thanks: Thank God for your own faith story.

Reflect: What new implications for your faith are you discovering through reading this book?

Explore: Read 1 Corinthians 15:3–7. We explored the whole chapter earlier in this section, but now just look at these few verses. They form one of the earliest 'creeds' – an affirmation of the Christian faith. The word 'creed' means 'I believe'. The creeds set out the boundaries of faith. We find credal statements like this in the Bible, and in later centuries there were questions and answers for people at their baptism, based upon the basic Christian beliefs. Eventually the creeds as we find them in many acts of worship came to be written. Borrow a service book from church and have a look at one of them. The two most well-known creeds are the Apostles' Creed and the Nicene Creed.

Pray: Jesus, help me to be a witness to the gospel.

Peter's shadow

Now many signs and wonders were done among the people
through the apostles. And they were all together in Solomon's
Portico. None of the rest dared to join them, but the people
held them in high esteem. Yet more than ever believers were
added to the Lord, great numbers of both men and women,
so that they even carried out the sick into the streets, and laid
them on cots and mats, in order that Peter's shadow might
fall on some of them as he came by. A great number of people
would also gather from the towns around Jerusalem, bringing the sick and those tormented by unclean spirits, and they
were all cured.

ACTS 5:12–16

These few verses are some of my favourites in the whole Bible. Their
beguiling simplicity is such that it is easy to overlook the huge significance of what is being said, for here we encounter the completely
transformed Peter.

First of all, we are told that many signs and wonders are being done
by the apostles, that they are held in high esteem by the people, and
that more and more are being added to the number of believers each
day. Here is a picture of the infant church bursting into life. The integrity and authenticity of the disciples' lives mean that people have
regard for them. The Holy Spirit is at work through them and people
are affirmed, forgiven and healed. The church's numbers are growing.

Then there is this amazing little sentence: 'They even carried out the
sick into the streets, and laid them on cots and mats, in order that
Peter's shadow might fall on some of them as he came by.'

It would be easy to pass this sentence by without realising what is being said. Having travelled with Peter through this book, we might be inclined to ask if this can be the same person – the same cocksure, foolhardy Peter who promised so much and delivered so little.

But it is the same Peter – Peter who has become the rock, because his life is now centred and built on Christ. He has become the Peter he was always capable of becoming. In Christ he has become himself. As a result, his life is completely focused on Christ and people see in him a radiant holiness that reflects the light of the risen Christ. It is so impressive and magnetic that people bring out the sick and those in need and lay them on the pavement, believing that even his passing shadow will bring a blessing.

Being a blessing

How would it be if people said the same sort of thing of us – that our lives so reflected the love of Christ that just our presence, our shadow, could bless and heal?

The bottom line of this book is that this can be so. If it can happen to Peter, it can happen to anyone! God can and will work out his purposes in our lives, and he can and will use us to bring his blessing to the world. He will not force himself upon us, though. He will wait for us to cooperate with his will. Therefore we need to walk in the light of Christ.

We need to be 'eccentric' Christians – not in the way the word is usually used, to mean someone a little crazy, but in the more literal sense of having our centre outside ourselves. This is what happens to Peter after the resurrection, after his restoration and through the gift of the Spirit. Jesus is the centre of Peter's life. Peter can be the rock for others only because he is so firmly built on Christ.

Now Peter walks down the street and there is almost a sense in which he doesn't notice the sick and the lame laid out on the pavement; not because he doesn't care but because he is focused on Christ, walking towards the light. Moreover, it might be to our benefit that we don't always see the results of our ministry. What is lovely about the image of the passing shadow is that we don't always see where it falls. Peter walks down the street, focused on Christ, and, as he goes about the business of being the person God has called him to be, so he becomes a blessing to others and a channel of grace. Often he will not be aware of the good that is being done through him. For someone like Peter, this was probably very important. As we know, he could so easily give in to pride and impetuosity, and he might have got some very funny ideas about himself if he saw what was happening because of his ministry. He might have started to imagine that it was down to him rather than the love of Christ at work through him.

Are we really so different from Peter? Once again, isn't the attraction of Peter the fact that he is so very human, so very much like us? Consequently, God does not always show us the fruits of our ministry. Rather, he asks us to be faithful and to walk in the way of Christ all the days of our lives. Our ministry will flow from our faithfulness as God puts before us opportunities to do his will and to show his way. Be sure of this: if you walk in the light you will cast a long shadow.

For reflection and prayer

Give thanks: Thank God for the many lives that you have touched and will touch in the future because of your faith in Christ, even if you do not know about it.

Reflect: How can you become more focused on Christ each day, so that your life casts a long shadow?

Explore: Read 2 Corinthians 4. Paul speaks of the light of Christ shining in us. He also speaks about persevering in ministry, of walking the way of faith.

Pray: Generous God, make my life a blessing to others.

Living stones

Come to him, a living stone, though rejected by mortals yet chosen and precious in God's sight, and like living stones, let yourselves be built into a spiritual house, to be a holy priesthood, to offer spiritual sacrifices acceptable to God through Jesus Christ. For it stands in scripture:

'See, I am laying in Zion a stone, a cornerstone chosen and precious; and whoever believes in him will not be put to shame.'

To you then who believe, he is precious; but for those who do not believe, 'The stone that the builders rejected has become the very head of the corner', and 'A stone that makes them stumble, and a rock that makes them fall.'

They stumble because they disobey the word, as they were destined to do. But you are a chosen race, a royal priesthood, a holy nation, God's own people, in order that you may proclaim the mighty acts of him who called you out of darkness into his marvellous light.

1 PETER 2:4–9

We end with this beautiful passage from the first letter of Peter, describing Jesus as the cornerstone of our faith, the one who was rejected, who has become the head of the corner. There is also an invitation: we can be living stones in the temple of God.

For nine years I lived in West Yorkshire, where the hills of the Pennines are chequered with dry-stone walls. Making these walls is quite an art. It is also very hard work. Therefore, whenever the dry-stone waller reaches down to pick up a stone, he always finds a place for it in the wall. He never rejects it or replaces it. Each stone picked up is elect and precious, and it is his job to find the right place for it, the place where it fits.

In the same way, we must allow ourselves to be picked up by God and used in the way he thinks fit. Together all of us form a great spiritual house. Beneath us is the witness of saints and apostles who have gone before us in the faith and brought us into the church. Jesus himself is the foundation.

Built into a spiritual house

Ministry belongs to the whole church. Together we bear witness to the gospel, interacting with one another and supporting one another. Everyone has a place within this great work, even though some, preferring the way of the world, find the rock, which is our security, a stone to stumble against. But God expends himself on this great work, longing to bring the whole creation into the recreated light of the kingdom.

Throughout this book we have seen how the pattern of God's call and our response is worked out in the life of Peter. As we have done this, we have seen how the Bible can speak to us, shaping and guiding our lives as disciples of Jesus. We need to go on drinking deeply from the well of scripture, for these words, written by those who felt the pull of God in the past, lead us to the living Word, the one who calls to us today.

As we have looked at Peter, we have also seen ourselves – our fervent desire to be great champions of the gospel, but also the transparent selfishness of these desires and the failures that go with them. In a strange way, the all-too-evident weaknesses of Peter are what make him such an attractive companion in our spiritual life. He is so like us, but he also demonstrates what God can do.

God has a picture in his heart of what our lives can become. In Peter this potential was fulfilled. The same possibility is available to us as we travel the way of faith, allowing God's grace and mercy to shape our living.

Legend has it that Peter was martyred in Rome, crucified upside down, because in the end he did not feel worthy even to share the same death as Jesus. But the story is also told that on the night before his execution he escaped from prison and fled along the Appian Way, out of Rome. On the path he met a familiar figure carrying a cross. It was Jesus.

'Where are you going, Lord?' Peter asked.

'I am going to Rome to be crucified again,' Jesus replied.

Peter turned, went back to the prison and was crucified the next day; taken where he did not want to go, but in the end faithful to his vocation, steadfast in his ministry, a true friend of Jesus.

For reflection and prayer

Give thanks: Thank God for St Peter, the rock, and for all the saints who show us how to be Christian.

Reflect: How will you continue reading the Bible on a regular basis?

Explore: Read Ephesians 2:11–21, another passage about being built together into a new humanity as the household of God, built upon the cornerstone of Christ.

Pray: Loving God, help me to be a true friend of Jesus; as you once did with Peter, turn my life around – turn me into my true self.

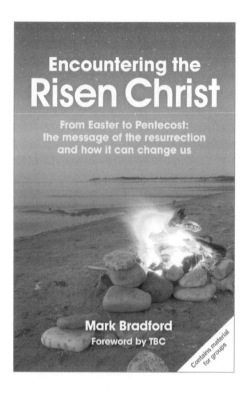

Encountering the
Risen Christ
From Easter to Pentecost:
the message of the resurrection
and how it can change us

Mark Bradford
Foreword by TBC

Contains material
for groups

The post-resurrection encounters between Jesus and the disciples provide us with some of the most profound and personal moments to be found in scripture. *Encountering the Risen Christ* reflects on the main characters in the post-resurrection accounts and shows how we too can encounter Jesus Christ in a life-transforming way. The seven chapters plus discussion material can be used across the seven weeks from Easter to Pentecost in individual reflection or group study, or at any time of year.

Encountering the Risen Christ
From Easter to Pentecost: the message of the resurrection and how it can change us
Mark Bradford
978 0 85746 428 6 £8.99

brfonline.org.uk

Guidelines is a unique Bible reading resource that offers four months of in-depth study, drawing on the insights of current scholarship. Its intention is to enable all its readers to interpret and apply the biblical text with confidence in today's world, while helping to equip church leaders as they meet the challenges of mission and disciple-building.

Guidelines

Bible study for today's mission and ministry
Edited by Helen Paynter and David Spriggs
£4.70 per issue or £17.85 for a year-long subscription

brfonline.org.uk/guidelines

Enabling all ages to grow in faith

Anna Chaplaincy
Living Faith
Messy Church
Parenting for Faith

The Bible Reading Fellowship (BRF) is a Christian charity that resources individuals and churches. Our vision is to enable people of all ages to grow in faith and understanding of the Bible and to see more people equipped to exercise their gifts in leadership and ministry.

To find out more about our ministries, visit
brf.org.uk